Psalms
in the Key
of Life

*A Look at African American
Spirituals and Hymns
as Pastoral Care Tools
in Crisis Counseling*

DR. CHARLES C. MARTIN SR.

PSALMS IN THE KEY OF LIFE
*A Look at African American Spirituals and Hymns
as Pastoral Care Tools in Crisis Counseling*

Copyright © 2025
by Dr. Charles C. Martin Sr.

ISBN: 978-1-7357848-1-6

Scripture is taken from the King James Version, public domain.

CONTACT INFORMATION

Email . . . . drmartin@charlesmartinministries.org

Web Page . . . . www.charlesmartinministries.org

Mailing . . . . P. O. Box 1062 • Cedar Hill, Texas 75106

DEDICATION

To my wife of thirty-five years,
Dr. Earlene Brown Martin
August 1947–April 2019

For thirty-five years you were my top fan, primary inspiration, and motivator. Your encouragement propelled me through difficult times, disappointments and personal struggles. As in the psalms of lament, you helped me to face my pain, crisis, or struggle and resolve to trust God regardless. As you always said, when trusting God, things get "gooderer and gooderer."

Acknowledgments

Special thanks to:
My Children
Whittney, Brittney, Charles II, and Dominique

Inspirational Friends
Bishop Kevin and Dr. Linda Willis
New Life Church of Memphis, Tennessee

Dr. Wanda Davis
CEO Maturing, Overcoming, Disciples Ministry

My Editor
Linda Stubblefield

TABLE OF CONTENTS

PREFACE

*P*salms in the Key of Life: A Look at African American Spirituals and Hymns as Tools of Pastoral Care in Crisis is a book intended for people who are discerning a calling to serve in the ministry of pastoral care of the congregation. Whether serving as a lay pastor care provider or as one who has enter the ministry as a licensed or ordained minister, this book is designed to engage you in a study of the issue of crisis in the lives of parishioners in the local church and the broader community.

In a course on "Ministry in Times of Crisis," the discussions addressed the reality of crisis that occurs in everyday life. Particular attention was given to looking at the development of crisis within the individual and examination of the actual element that precipitated the actual crisis environment or situation.

Howard Stone, in his book *Crisis Counseling*, states: "An outside precipitator or emotional hazard, such as death, divorce, or job loss, usually triggers crisis; these precipitators are always situational and frequently interpersonal in nature."[1]

Stone suggests that in crisis intervention giving attention to the precipitator, the cause of the crisis, is important. In this way, both the individual in crisis and the intervener are adequately informed and able to determine the proper methods of intervention. Stone goes on to suggest that individuals experience crises when a loss is perceived or threatened. "The loss can be of a significant person, a love or dependency relationship, financial support, health, life, a family role a sense of worthfulness, values, or meaning of life. Losses do not necessarily occur only in the form of divorce or death."[2]

It is the losses in life that I believe precipitate the crisis of grief. At the point of wrestling with the grief crisis, individuals who are experiencing emotions, frustrations, despair etc., seek to find coping mechanisms for their grief. Donald Capps suggests in his book, *Biblical Approaches to Pastoral Counseling*, that the Psalms are viable tools or resources for working with people in situations of grief. He references the work of authors Sweard Hiltner, Wayne Oates and Carroll Wise to support his position regarding the use of the Psalms and particularly Psalms of Lament. He states the following:

> A major reason for their emphasis on the psalms is the psalms' reflection of human emotional experience, and for these authors, pastoral counseling aims to help counselees express and clarify their feelings. By "feelings," they do not mean emotions that come and go, but deep feelings that reflect serious intrapsychic conflicts.[3]

Capps emphasizes the validity of the lamentable psalms as practical tools for individuals regardless of the precipitator of the crisis. It is with these ideas in mind that this book is conceived.

In this book I intend to focus on the method of intervention used historically in the African American church and community in dealing with crisis. I identify the crisis as grief and the precipitator of the crisis as loss. I refer to grief in this book with respect to the losses in life encountered by individuals in the African American community and not only the perspective of death. These losses resulted in great lament for those grieving and may be comparable to the laments as expressed in the psalms. I will explore this possibility in the development of this work with respect to the relationship of the Psalms of lament and the expressions found in African American Spirituals and Hymns.

In writing this book, it is my hope that it will serve as a tool to equip the reader with a better understanding of the grief process and the effectiveness or ineffectiveness of Spirituals and Hymns as tools of intervention. *In this work I will:*

A. Reflect historically upon the development of African American Spirituals and Hymns and identify the difference between Spirituals and Hymns.

B. Reflect on the Theology of African American Spirituals and Hymns and the grief process found in Psalms. Using this, I will explore the relationship of Psalms to Spirituals and Hymns as a crisis intervention tool with grief.

C. Discover the ways in which Spirituals and Hymns assist as an intervention tool for individuals who have experienced the crisis of grief and critically assess how Spirituals and Hymns assist as intervention tools.

D. Evaluate the effectiveness of Spirituals and Hymns in grief crisis interventions in the African American church.

To accomplish this goal, I will:

A. Research and discuss the Development of African American Spirituals and Hymns and define the difference between Spirituals and Hymns in the African American Church.

B. Compare the relationship between the use of the Psalms in grief intervention with the use of Spirituals and Hymns in grief intervention.

C. Formulate and administer a questionnaire to be given to the congregation to evaluate the use of Spirituals and Hymns as coping mechanisms by individuals in grief situations.

D. Discern the use of Spirituals and Hymns in the African American Church today, and using responses from the questionnaire, include a summary on "Spirituals and Hymns as Pastoral Care Tools in Crisis Intervention."

INTRODUCTION

Since December of 1986, I have served as the senior pastor of the Union Missionary Baptist Church in Dallas, Texas. In the years of my tenure, I have encountered many situations of grief with parishioners ranging from death, divorce, separation, job losses, and more. The dynamics of each loss are similar and just as much a crisis as any other extreme or catastrophic loss. The history of the African American church is rich with the use of music and particularly hymns and spirituals, which have served as a coping mechanism for many in crisis situations.

In this book I will seek to examine the use of spirituals and hymns to discover the ways in which they were instrumental in healing and intervening in crisis times. The question I seek to answer is, "How can these tools be used today as a tool of pastoral care in crisis situations?" My theological understanding is that one of the responsibilities of the pastor is to shepherd the flock of God, which includes rendering assistance and guidance in times of crisis. The admonition of the apostle Paul supports this idea: *"Now we exhort you, brethren, warm them that are unruly, comfort the feebleminded, support the weak, be patient toward all men"* (1 Thessalonians 5:14).

In this work, I seek to focus on the method of intervention used historically in the African American church and community in dealing with crisis. I identify the crisis as grief and the precipitator of the crisis as loss. My reference to grief in this project is with respect to the overall losses in life encountered by individuals in the African American community, not only the experience of loss resulting from death.

Although the context of this work is the African American community, the reader will find helpful information for ministry in any racially diverse context. This work examines the use of hymns and spirituals as tools of pastoral care when assisting individuals with grief and other crisis, while making comparison with the Psalms of lament and given in the Bible.

Historical pastoral care and its development will be explored in the African American church and community. Finally, this work guides the reader in thoughtful reflection of the traditional approach of pastoral care in crisis situations and a reevaluation of its methods.

As pastoral caregivers develop a greater awareness of the context of care and the context of the individual care seeker, the ministry of pastoral care and its methods employed will have a greater effect. This effect will communicate to care seekers the boundless love of God as demonstrated by the people of God through the caring ministry of the church.

THE DEVELOPMENT OF AFRICAN AMERICAN SPIRITUALS AND HYMNS

The African American community maintains a rich history consisting of the use of various forms of music in a myriad of situations and circumstances. Music is germane to the African American community. Music represents a language, a desire, a motivation, a spirit and a story for African Americans. James Cone conveys this idea when he says, "Black music is unifying because it confronts the individual with the truth of black existence and affirms that being black is possible only in a communal context."[1]

Music in the African American church is designed to build up the body of Christ while also identifying the individual as a part of the larger context of community. J. Wendell Mapson Jr. states the following:

> No doubt music will always be a vital component of the religious pilgrimage of black Americans. As it has done in the past, music must continue to comment on the hopes, fears, disappointments, and faith of a people who still must struggle to "Sing the Lord's song in a strange land."[2]

This look at music in the African American community can be very broad and extensive and therefore I seek to confine my discussion to the realm of the music of the African American church referred to as spirituals and hymns. Because of the significance and meaning music has in the African American community I will, of necessity, refer to some secular instances of the use of music to establish my position. Furthermore, I seek to discuss the development of African American spirituals and hymns and identify the difference between these two styles of music. To accomplish this objective, I will give a brief historical perspective on the significance of music as it relates to the African American community and explore its theological meanings for the community. Having done this, I will seek to follow and revisit the early development of the music referred to as spirituals and hymns to discover their origin and uniqueness.

Looking Back: A Historical Perspective
Beginning with the Slavery Period

> The African American church begins in slavery; so, slave religion provides the first source for a constructive statement on a black theology of liberation. The black church's unique tradition springs from the emerging theology of African American chattel. Enslaved African Americans creatively forged their own understanding of God, Jesus Christ, and the purpose of humanity. Through scriptural insights, theological imagination, and direct contact with God, black bondsmen and bondswomen combined faith instincts from their African traditional religions with the justice message of the Christian Gospel and planted seeds for a black theology expressed through politics and culture. This practical and sacred worldview evolved into an institutional worship setting under bondage.[3]

This statement by Dwight N. Hopkins helps to set the tone and direction of this portion of this discussion. It is suggestive of the foundations of faith and understanding as possessed by the African slaves as they lived in a difficult and dehumanizing environment. Amid this kind of situation, the African slaves held fast to their worship. An integral part of their worship experience was music, the singing of the songs of their home, culture and beliefs.

In many instances, their songs preserved their identity and uniqueness as individuals and as a community of exiles. African slaves brought with them intrinsic characteristics of a culture which could not and would not be extinguished in a new land. In his book *Negro Slave Songs in the United States,* Miles Mark Fisher identifies some of the characteristics of African culture, especially as they relate to the music and worship practices of the African. Of particular importance was the fact that religion, as well as music, was deeply embedded in the whole of African life. It is noted that the African's view of the world was holistic. Their view focused upon being in relationship with one another and with the whole of creation.[4]

In African life and tradition, music played a part in every event and experience. Music revealed the unwritten stories of the history of a given community. Because of the place of music in African life and culture, it is no surprise that slaves in America retained their culture, history and beliefs through their music. Regardless of their oppression and imprisonment, the music of the people could not be destroyed even as Africans were brought into a New World. This exile and dislocation of the Africans from their homeland meant "singing their song in a strange land." Thus, the African slaves adapted to their new environment but never accepted their relegated place or status in the New World.

This fact is made evident in the music of the slaves as they sought to maintain a means of communicating with each other. Throughout this struggle for identity, freedom, and recognition, the slaves endeavored to maintain a sense of their community, religious beliefs and hope as they forced themselves to adapt to their new environment.

Having looked at a brief history of the period of slavery and the music of the African people, let us consider now the transitioning of music in the African American community both sacred and secular.

Transitioning of Music in the African American Community

I use the term "transitioning" to refer to the transformation and development of the music of Africans into the music of African Americans. I cite here not only the words of the music, but also the "being" of the music. The music had personality as the people who sang the songs embodied it. The music of the people was first African. However, having been relocated to a new place and experiencing the diaspora of African people into America, the music became the music of African Americans.

Here I am suggesting a view which identifies the cultural distinctiveness of African music now transformed and stained by the pains, struggles, hurts, and experiences of a people who once lived life free but now struggle to realize liberation again. In this transformation or transition, songs that spoke of tribal hunting and celebration of the catch would now become songs of pain as the hunted and captured. Songs that celebrated history and family would now long for family and reflect on its history.

Songs of worship were now forged out of the misery and pains associated with the dehumanization of the slaves and their struggle to regain identity as a great people created by God. Music became an indispensable vehicle used by the slaves, through which they could travel safely in the song across the land without the fear of being captured.

Because of the coded messages in the songs, the slave masters could not prevent the "musical flight" of the slaves from one place to another. The song could not be captured or held in stocks. Music represented freedom and hope.

The improvisation of Africans and African Americans in music is indicative of the plight of slaves to have freedom despite their present oppressive circumstances. The Africans slaves developed many ways to improvise in life regardless of their present condition. in his book, *Shoes That Fit Our Feet*, Dwight N. Hopkins references the efforts of African Americans to "get over" on their masters. This undertaking is exemplified in African folklore and African work songs.

One such example Hopkins mentions is found in the thought of the Africans as it is presented in the idea of the *Way Maker* or *Way Made*. This concept represents the ultimate realized hope enjoyed by the poor and enslaved, where they reach their true selves and come to their final space. Hopkins identifies three ways in African American folk culture that voiceless black people participated in the fruits of the *Way Maker* or *Way Made* in reclaiming their God-given humanity. These three ways are 1) song, 2) having fun, and 3) the ancestors.[5]

To emphasize this point and further illustrate the idea of transitioning, observe the following excerpt from Hopkins regarding *song*:

> During the antebellum period, a certain peg-leg sailor known as Peg-Leg Joe developed a "secular" song that, in fact, served as a thread to the slaves' faith movement to a stolen freedom. Calling the song "Foller de Drinkin' Gou'd," Joe told how the Big Dipper (the Drinkin' Gou'd) would help escaping chattel pursue northern direction under the cover of night. Joe would show slaves the imprints that his natural peg-leg made so that, after he had departed, bondswomen and bondsmen could

track him to emancipation by both the stars and his footprints. The trickster Peg-Leg Joe uses the language of nature in the song both to protect and free black chattel. Particularly, the escaping African American deploys a double-faced mask while singing. On the one hand, white slaveowners and accommodating blacks (both representing satanic enforcers of bound human flesh) would interpret the lyrics sung as, perhaps, happy darkies idling their time away. Natural metaphors flood the entire song and bring to mind rhythmic servants engrossed in the idyllic or pastoral. The surface interpretation by the enemy greatly aided slave strategy for deliverance, for it deflected any suspicion away from their subtextual intent. A faith song, therefore, serves to sidetrack and befuddle satanic opponents of an emancipatory journey...The song contains coded language, which only those of faith hear and perceive...This secular liberation song encouraged enslaved African Americans to risk life and death for their ultimate Way Made – a chance for a peaceful unchained identity and unrestrained mobility. Their precarious non-guaranteed act, hence a step marked by a faith leap, indicates their unwavering conviction to sing their way to a promised land up north.[6]

This excerpt illustrates the way the music of Africans made transitions to adjust to and provide a way through the conditions of which they were now a part. It represents the dual meanings often found in the music of African Americans. The transitioning of the music was a way of continuing to have community and relationship with the larger African American community. This also reveals the significance of the song and music in the African American community.

THE SIGNIFICANCE OF MUSIC
IN THE AFRICAN AMERICAN COMMUNITY

Music or *Song* continues to be a viable force in the lives of African Americans. As it was a voice of hope during the era of slavery and oppression, it continues. Whether secular or spiritual, *song* exists as a viable life source within the African American community.

The first music or songs sung in the African American church were informal songs that Eileen Southern, John Lovell and Wyatt Tee Walker call *field chants, field hollers, work songs,* and *moans.*

> These genres are the parents and godparents to what later evolved into the African American spirituals. The first protest uttered musically whether in the bowels of a slave ship or under the hot sun—whether in the slave quarters or in the big house of the Caribbean—whether verbal, coded or sung openly, birthed a new genre of music that has never been heard before and had never been heard before in the Western Hemisphere.[7]

With these thoughts in mind, it is no surprise that the music of the African Americans maintained a link for the Africans with their homeland and with fellow Africans scattered in their new environment. Whether the slaves were in the Northern States, Southern States, Cuba, or any other location, their vinculum—their music and singing—was the same. In his book, *The Spirituals and the Blues,* James Cone gives five statements describing black music:
1) Black music is unity music.
2) Black music is functional.
3) Black music is a living reality.
4) Black music is social and political.
5) Black music is theological.

These statements in my view encompass the existential nature of the music of African Americans. Cone discusses each of these statements and gives meaning to each considering his perspective on the relationship of the spirituals and the blues. I will endeavor to relate them to the overall significance as it relates to African Americans in my discussion. Furthermore, you will also observe in this section my use of both terms *African* and *Black* in reference to the same community.

The significance of black music being *unity music* suggests its indigenous ability to link together a people whether they are together or apart. It is a statement that suggests the idea of community that exists on a level that is deeper than surface ties. It speaks of a relationship that exists between people that is unbound and unbroken. Cone states, "It unites the joy and the sorrow, the love and the hate, the hope and the despair of black people; and it moves people toward the direction of total liberation."[8]

Black music being *functional* suggests a degree of flexibility. Many of the songs had double and even triple meanings. The meaning of a song is derived only from the context in which the song is sung or from the situation the individual is experiencing. In the mind of the African and African Americans, the music is the same regardless of the genre or label attached to it. The same beat which motivates movement and dance in the clubs or at the party, is also used in worship. The European culture sought in ways to eliminate this functional aspect of African music in the worship because it was not deemed to be sacred. However, regardless of the attempt to change this view, African American music retains a very functional nature within the community. On this note, James Cone says, "Its purposes and aims are directly related to the consciousness of the black community. To be functional is to be useful in community definition, style, and movement."[9]

As a *living reality*, black music addresses the plight, problems, so-

lutions and joys of being black. It voices the paradoxes of life and illustrates the issues of relational life and its difficulties. It reveals the
truth of the experiences of black people and operates as a vehicle of
communication to give an interpretation to one's experiences in life.

The *social and political* character reveal the individual's views regarding their status in dealing with their oppressor and the values
which were being driven into the slaves to accept. Furthermore, careful listening to the songs of African Americans will uncover clues as
to what is happening to them sociologically. Cone says, "It is social
because it is black and thus articulates the separateness of the black
community...It is political because in its rejection of white cultural
values, it affirms the political otherness of black people."[10]

Black music disclosed a different view of life that stood in contra-
diction to the established law, and beliefs of white society; therefore,
the individual and the community retained its uniqueness and identity
as a people without being engulfed in a cultural exchange in which all
sense of heritage and ethnicity are lost.

The *theological* nature of black music communicates the presence
and activity of God in every event of black life. The theological nature
reflects beliefs that came with the Africans from their native land. In
many ways it depicted their view of God in everything, their beliefs
regarding nature, life, and issues concerning suffering and death. This
view suggests that there is almost always a spiritual component in the
music of African Americans which reflect certain theological beliefs.
Whether gospel, blues, folk, or work song the theological dimension
remains an ever-present reality.

To summarize these views regarding the significance of music in
the African American community, I suggest that because music or
song was an ever-present part of life for the African, much of the theology of African Americans is revealed in the songs. In many ways

the theology of the African is basically a theology of liberation. In the secret meetings of the slaves when they gathered illegally to worship, they created a coherent and dynamic theology. Dwight Hopkins makes a very significant assertion regarding slave theology as he uncovers the theology of the African American today:

> Slave theology employed metaphors for both Jesus' kingly and priestly offices and Jesus' attributes of friend and mother. Black theology in slave religious experiences required such descriptions because slaves needed hope in their warfare against evil visible principalities and powers; they had to have the nurturing of friendship and wisdom.[11]

Inherent in the theological nature is also revealed the significance of music in the African experience and the African American church. Music was the vehicle through which such metaphors and theological beliefs were expressed. As stated previously, music has always been a vital ingredient within the existence of the African community and served as a valuable means of communicating hopes and dreams for their future. Communicating these hopes was developed into an oral tradition that was passed on to generations through the songs of the people. Dr. Wyatt Tee Walker speaks regarding the significance of music as it relates to oral tradition and says,

> To understand the depth and deep rootedness of the oral tradition, one must appreciate several facts about African life that not only antedate the Atlantic slave trade but are also apparent today…African history is preserved in its music. Within the context of the holistic theological systems of Africa, all life is manifestly religious. The events of life—birth, death, puberty, fertility, harvest, famine, marriage, tragedy—have religious rites that give expression to that event. In the absence of any

prescribed formula as to what is done and when, the music and the companion ceremony have been the key to the orchestration of events and the primary preservative ingredient of tradition.[12]

This excerpt identifies the significance of and primary role of music in the life of the African community. This music that was indigenous to the African in the past, remains to the African American community of today. However, in addition to this, music was a source of teaching and learning for the African. History reveals that some slaves were permitted to attend worship with their masters seated in a section reserved for them. There they heard the message of the Scriptures proclaimed. Having heard the scriptures in the church, and as they heard the stories of the bible taught to the children in the "big house," they began to share the messages with other field slaves.

Upon learning the stories of the oppressed people of God, the slaves began to see themselves as a parallel story. They believed in a God Who was on the side of the oppressed, a God Who would bring about the liberation of his people. They identified with the sufferings of Israel and the many servants of God through their slavery and persecution. Music, therefore, served to inspire or cause the fire of hope to continue to burn deep within the hearts of Africans everywhere. Combined with the inherent significance of music and their understanding of God, the music underwent a change to express the experiences of the slaves.

THE DEVELOPMENT OF HYMNS AND SPIRITUALS IN THE AFRICAN AMERICAN COMMUNITY

The conditions of slaves in the New World made it impossible for the slaves to share the hopes, dreams, and desires they had for a better future. Considering this, the slaves developed another means of communicating their hopes and dreams. Once slaves were given access to the Bible and learned to read the stories of the Scriptures, their hopes were revived. Northern slaves and freedmen who enjoyed liberties not afforded to slaves in other regions including the South, were able to attend worship with their masters. They were segregated; however, they heard and sang the same songs of the church sung by their masters.

During this time a British influence prevailed upon the church, resulting in a certain type of worship and music that was deemed acceptable. The music of this worship constituted the early hymns. These hymns sung in the church were the acceptable form of musical expression in the church. In seeking to define this form of church music, the following information was gathered. Hymns as we know them today could be deemed as songs of praise and adoration to God as sung by people of God. Willi Apel suggests, "In the early Christian era, the term *hymn* was applied to all songs in praise of the Lord."[13]

The *Larousse Encyclopedia of Music* states the following regarding the hymn:

> The definition of the hymn has presented difficulties since the earliest times. For St. Augustine it was "the praise of God by singing." If one of the three elements implied in this definition—namely, praise, devotion to God, or song—is lacking, then there is, according to Augustine, no hymn. But this definition also covers psalms and canticles, and we can further define the hymn if we add a fourth necessary element—that it should be sung by the congregation.[14]

This definition of *hymn* reflects the views held by many Anglos concerning hymnology and its sacredness in the church. Since the influence on the church and its worship was largely Anglican, this definition remained. History suggests that the freedom of many slaves to participate in corporate worship experiences brought about many changes. Eileen Southern states the following:

> During the 1730's the "Great Awakening" movement brought with it a demand for the use of "livelier" music (than the psalms and canticles) in the worship service. These new "livelier" songs were called hymns. This new style of texts by Dr. Isaac Watts (1647-1748) and Charles Wesley (1707-1788) appealed to Blacks because of the vitality of the words, the wider use of intervals than in the psalm tunes, and their rhythmic freedom.[15]

This quote presents the hymn as more than meeting the criteria imposed by Augustine and goes further to represent hymns also as a more spirited genre of music, which resulted in a different response for those who sang them in worship. The fact that these hymns were livelier songs was appealing to the African American, which also meant that they were therefore more readily adopted by African Americans to be used in their worship.

Some writers attribute the life and vigor of the hymns in White churches, although segregated, to the presence and involvement of the slaves in the singing of the songs of the church. J. Jefferson Cleveland suggests that in the latter part of the eighteenth century, blacks began to break away from the predominately white congregations to establish their own places of worship. In the process of establishing churches for themselves, blacks also brought along the ideas of worship and music which they had observed in the White churches, thus bringing into their own worship a semblance of the White church. Considering the fact of blacks being able to have their own worship Cleveland goes on to say:

When blacks began to establish their own churches, they did not discard the sophisticated hymns learned from their experiences in White Christian worship; rather, many of these hymns were adopted and converted into original black songs. These "made-over" White hymns were the result of diverse influences including: (1) African religious music, (2) the African call-and-response song, (3) European or African religious and secular songs, and (4) various African and Afro-American dialectics.[16]

Based upon the information provided by scholars, the aforementioned served as the process through which hymns were developed in the African American church. Not until the twentieth century was there any emergence of African American composers or authors of hymns used in the church. Most of these songs used were rearrangements and compositions of early hymns rewritten in the flavor and zeal of the African American community. Dr. Charles Albert Tindley was the most renowned and prolific of the Black hymn writers. Tony Heilbut states,

> Tindley's gospel hymns compromised an entirely new genre, and he admitted that they leaned heavily on the Negro spiritual. Tindley incorporated folk images, proverbs, and biblical allusions well known to Black Christians for over a hundred years; yet his songs had a profound universal appeal to the human heart, with words of hope, cheer, love, and pity.[17]

One of the hymns or so-called "gospel hymns" written by Tindley[18] is "The Storm is Passing Over."

Courage, my soul, and let us journey on,
Tho' the night is dark it won't be very long...

REFRAIN:
Hallelujah! Hallelujah! The storm is passing over, Hallelujah.

The poor and downtrodden, and those bending beneath the weight of cares have often found solace in Tindley's song "Leave It There."

Leave it there, leave it there,
Take your burden to the Lord and leave it there,
If you trust and never doubt, He will surely bring you out,
Take your burden to the Lord and leave it there.

The rearranging of many of the hymns of the Anglican Church in the African American church gave the hymns an expression indicative only of the experiences and life of the African American community. These hymns found their way into the worship of the black church because of the theology of the black church and theological views that were revealed in the hymns. Additionally, the rhythm, movements, beats, and coded meanings prevalent with the spirituals was added to the understanding and singing of these songs.

In summary, these definitions and interpretations of hymns shed light upon the evolution and use of hymns in the African American church. Furthermore, the influence of the White church's impact on the lives of the African slaves can be established. This impact served as a type of model for many of the slaves in adopting the style of worship deemed appropriate by their white counterparts.

Although this style conflicted with the cultural heritage of the African slave in worship, it was deemed appropriate especially by slaves in the north. The slaves in the South, however, were not impacted in the same manner as their brothers and sisters in other areas. The fact that slavery in the South was primarily agricultural, plantations usually had several slaves, and therefore slave owners did not allow the slaves to attend worship with them. Instead, the slaves gathered in a church named for the slave owner (such as Brown's Chapel) or worshipped together in secret in what became known as the "invisible church." These invisible churches were secret places where the slaves gathered in secret and held worship services. Apart from their European influence, the songs of the "invisible church" largely influenced the hymns of the African American church. These songs, field hollers, moans, work songs, or sorrow songs are the songs that are known as the "spirituals."

The Development of the Spirituals

According to many African American historians and writers, the spirituals emanated from the heart of the antebellum Negro slave as forceful eruptions of religious passion. These spirituals were birthed through the pains and sufferings of the slaves whose desire was to once again be free. Most writers agree that the spirituals are unique to the Americanization of the African. The spirituals were not products of their African homeland; rather, they were shaped, inspired by, and developed through the experience of slavery. Yet they also stand as a remarkable contribution to music given by African Americans. J. Wendell MapsonJr. states the following:

> The spirituals are a distinctly American contribution, not born in Africa. Emerging out of the experience of a people in slavery, the spirituals told the story of a disenfranchised people. The spirituals expressed the full range of human emotion: pain, fear, joy, sorrow, despair, hope, futility, and faith. These "sorrow songs" as spirituals are also called, told the bittersweet story of hardship and struggle. The music of the slaves became the medium by which they were able to survive. The slaves never accepted slavery, and the spirituals, punctuated with hope, are testimonies of the yearning within human souls to be free.[19]

J. Jefferson Cleveland offers these words regarding the meaning and development of the spirituals:

These songs—variously called Negro spirituals, jubilees, folk songs, shout songs, sorrow songs, slave songs, slave melodies, minstrel songs, and religious songs—are most commonly known as Negro spirituals because of the deep religious feeling they express. Many of these spirituals were influenced by the surrounding conditions in which the slaves lived. The spirituals, which speak of life and death, suffering and sorrow, love and judgment, grace and hope, justice and mercy, were born out of this tradition. They are the songs of a people weary at heart. The Negro spirituals are the songs of an unhappy people, and yet they are the most beautiful expressions of human experience born this side of the seas.[20]

Black theologian James H. Cone suggests the following in relation to the development and inspiration of the spirituals:

The divine liberation of the oppressed from slavery is the central theological concept in the black spirituals. These songs show that black slaves did not believe that human servitude was reconcilable with their African past and their knowledge of the Christian gospel. They did not that God created Africans to be the slaves of Americans. Accordingly, they sang of a God who was involved in history—their history—making right what whites had made wrong. Just as God delivered the Children of Israel from Egyptian slavery, drowning Pharaoh and his army in the Red Sea, he will also deliver black people from American slavery. It is this certainty that informs the thought of the black spirituals, enabling black slaves to sing:

> *Oh, Mary, don't you weep, don't you moan,*
> *Oh, Mary, don't you weep, don't you moan,*

Pharaoh's army got drownded,
Oh, Mary, don't you weep.[21]

Other writers who speak to the subject of African American spirituals suggest that the spirituals are more "other worldly." The implication is that they are focused upon the repudiation of this world and its problems, finding hope only in aspirations of a better place where their desires are no longer denied. While I understand this view, I am an advocate of the view that spirituals contain many interpretations. The multi-coded nature of these spirituals allowed the slaves to possess the hope of a better place on earth—not just in the sweet by and by. My position is that the spirituals addressed life and all its extremities. The spirituals afforded the slaves the opportunity to blend their experiences into a message of hope, endurance, and survival. These songs found their basis in the Scriptures that the slaves heard, read, or in some way were made familiar to them. The vast number of scriptural references and scenes depicting God's involvement in the lives of His people fueled the passions and words of the Negro spirituals.

Howard Thurman suggests that the majority of the text came from the Old and New Testaments of the Holy Bible, yet the world of nature and the common personal experiences of religion also provided texts for these songs. Additionally, of importance to note is that the teachings of the Bible and Christianity played a significant part in the development of this musical style.

In summary, after taking a historical look at the music through the period of slavery and its relatedness to the life of the African community, the transitioning of the music of the African to the music of African Americans and tracing its changes and uniqueness was addressed. This analysis led us to look at the significance of music in the African American community to discover its meaning to the individual and the community and explored its theological meanings to the community. Finally, I sought in this essay to discuss the development of African American spirituals and hymns in the African American church and community. At this point, I want to suggest what I believe to be the difference or uniqueness of these two genres of music in the African American church.

Spirituals and hymns are related in the African American church by virtue of the community. The nature of the hymns was directed solely at praise, adoration, and worship. In the African American church these same hymns were rearranged to contain a personal note that made the message real to life circumstances and situations. The hymns of the church which were largely rearranged and later written by African Americans, voice the praise and worship of the community. The difference that exists between these two centers is the origin of each.

The spirituals were born in the bosom of African slaves and based primarily upon a liberation motif. This quality of the spirituals makes them the laments of the African American community. They reveal not only the voice and feelings of an individual but a community. The original hymns of the church were here and already being sung in the white church upon the arrival of the Africans in the New World. The spirituals are what I call the "musical children" given birth by African Americans to foster a hope for a new life in a hostile and unfriendly environment.

In concluding these thoughts, the words of the gospel of John chapter 1 come to mind. However, the words come to me as they relate to the music of hymns and spirituals in the African American church. Though not an accurate presentation of the gospel narrative, the music voices the feelings that flow in my heart as I ponder these significant contributions by my ancestors.

Dr. Charles C. Martin Sr.

————

In the beginning was the song,
The song was with the music,
The song was music,
In the song was life,
And the life was the light of hope.
The song became flesh and dwelt among us.[22]

African American Spirituals and Hymns and the Grief Process in the Psalms

The spirituals and hymns of the African American Church possess a certain quality and meaning within the African American Community which has allowed them to serve the community in a multifarious manner.

The Grief Process in Psalms, Spirituals and Hymns

Historical evidence reveals that these spirituals and hymns contained coded messages and multiple meanings regarding life and death, slavery and freedom, joy and suffering. Because of the many interpretations possible for these songs, they were also invaluable to the African American community in handling crisis, loss, and grief situations. The scope of crises, grief, and loss in the African American community is very broad and includes a wide range of experiences and grief precipitators. I acknowledge that these same situations are also true of many other communities and cultures; however, my focus is intentionally upon the African American church and community in America.

I will investigate the relationship of Psalms to spirituals and hymns in grief intervention first by examining the use of the Psalms in grief situations. I will then analyze the relationship of the Psalms with the African American spirituals and hymns. Finally, I will address their use as tools with individuals in grief situations as a stratagem to assist in crisis intervention. Through this process, my aim is to establish a view of the usefulness of African American spirituals and hymns as a helpful approach in crises. The approach I will take in my discussion will extend beyond a focus on death as the grief precipitator, to include other crises that also contribute to creating the feelings of grief in the life of the individual.

THE USE OF PSALMS IN GRIEF INTERVENTION
Grief

In undertaking this task to look at the use of the Psalms in grief intervention, I believe sharing some definitions of grief is necessary for understanding. The following meanings are helpful in giving clarity to my presentation. John W. James and Frank Cherry define *grief* in the *Grief Recovery Handbook* as follows:

- "A normal and natural response to loss."

- "The feeling of reaching out to someone who has always been there, only to find that when we need them one last time, they are no longer there."

- "A conflicting mass of human emotion that we experience following any major change in familiar pattern of behavior."[23]

It is no surprise or great revelation that everyone experiences feelings of grief. Regardless of age, status, gender, size, or ethnicity, grief is a normal part of human existence and the experience of life. Of these three definitions given by James and Cherry, the approach often receiving the most attention is the grief experience incurred at the loss of a loved one through death. Obviously, this particular area of study regarding grief is quite extensive. Viewing death as a great loss therefore creates a need to address other dynamics of grief.

Richard A. DeVaul and Sidney Zisook describe a three-stage process in dealing with grief consisting of 1) shock, 2) acute mourning, and 3) resolution.[24]

Dr. Howard Stone also conducted considerable empirical research in this area of grief. His study was conducted at the Los Angeles Suicide Prevention Center and focused upon death as the precipitator. In his research, he concludes that grief involves seven dynamics when dealing with the death of a loved one. He suggests these dynamics are also regarded as seven major elements typical of adapting to a great loss:

(1) *Shock*, marked by a period of numbness, the person being anesthetized against feeling the loss, (2) *catharsis*, the reality of the loss becoming apparent as the bereaved begins to release emotions, (3) *depression*, as the person alternates between periods of depression with feelings of anxiety, anger, and guilt, (4) *guilt* which varies in intensity from individual to individual, (5) *preoccupation* with the loss, (6) *anger*, indicating that the individual is coming out of the depression, and (7) *adaptation* to reality as the individual makes a new commitment to life, realizing the futility of continued withdrawal from reality.[25]

In identifying these seven elements, Dr. Stone seems to be stressing the idea that grief brings many strong emotions to the forefront. This dynamic could also be true regarding grief with other crises as the precipitator. Although this focus on the crisis or grief experience resulting from death is quite prevalent, in my research I have observed that many counselors and authors agree that a number of grief precipitators exist.

Furthermore, they also agree that grief itself finds expression in a variety of ways. Dr. Howard Clinebell states,

> Grief is involved in all significant changes, losses, and life transitions, not just in the death of a loved person. Every life event on the Holmes-Rahe stress scale involves some loss and therefore grieving.[26]

I must admit as I gave thought to this presentation that my initial thoughts were heavily influenced by the preponderance of information and discussions on grief relative to the death of a loved one. I found that in order to maintain the view of the broader dimensionality of grief, I had to maintain an intentional focus on the various issues or circumstances that create feelings of grief for an individual or community. The other two definitions given by James and Cherry concur with the view that grief is not limited to the experience of death and identify grief as an emotional response that creates a struggle within the individual.

My personal view is that grief is primarily a response to specific circumstances occurring in the life of an individual. The circumstance itself alters the homeostasis of the individual, resulting in feelings and responses indicative of grief. Grief then is "a response to circumstances or disruption of the normal balance of life for an individual or community." Throughout the remainder of this work, I shall refer to these circumstances as crises. Another word I wish to introduce at this time is the word *lament* to begin transition into our observation of the use of Psalms in grief intervention.

Lament

The word *lament* defined by the *Random House College Dictionary* is: "To feel or to express sorrow or regret for...to feel, show, or express grief, sorrow, or regret; to mourn deeply…an expression of grief or sorrow…a formal expression of sorrow or mourning, especially in verse or song; an elegy or dirge."[27]

This definition focuses on lament as an expression of grief, suggesting that lament is born out of the grief experience of an individual or community. This definition, however, also seems very limited in its explanation and in giving understanding for a better view of this word. This limited explanation appears to exist because it seems to focus only on one view of lamenting, leaving me with the impression of a person remaining in a constant state of grieving, mourning, and despair.

In his book, *Listening In: A Multicultural Reading of the Psalms,* Dr. Stephen Breck Reid suggests that laments have certain characteristics. For instance, he identifies *tenacity* as a characteristic of laments[28] that must be considered. He expresses the view that laments are stubborn and hard to get rid of like the tinsel from a Christmas tree. I am not fully able to embrace this view. If I understand the words of Dr. Reid correctly, he seemingly suggests that laments are persistent in forcing the individual to remain in a posture of grief, lamenting to the point of the individual's embodying his or her circumstance or situation. In addition, this view contends that the power of lamenting is overwhelming to the extent of dictating to the individual when its task has been completed.

I agree that taking time to lament is necessary; however, the quantity of time given is determined by the individual—not by the crises. In this sense, saying that a person has rushed too quickly to the "good news or happy times" if they have greeted their grief and finished their lament can be complex. Dr. Reid further suggests in his discussion on "What Makes a Lament," that three subjects dominate the laments in the Psalter: *"God, the one who laments, and the enemy."* He continues:

"The plot of the lament typically includes the reality of the Psalmist's alienation, conflict with another person(s), and a sense of the absence of the responsive God."[29]

To me, this quote speaks to an overwhelming sense of loss on the part of the individual or community that laments. I see the psalmist's alienation as his loss of peace; his conflict with another person(s) as loss of community; and his sense of the absence of his responsive God as loss of divine support. Losing each of these connections leaves the individual with a strong sense of loss, resulting in feelings of grief. Dr. Reid further suggests that laments begin with the realization that something is not right. This approach seems to be too vague and perhaps somewhat of a generalization of the origin of lament. This view gives the impression that circumstances cause the lament of the individual or community.

While I do not seek to be overly critical of the statement Dr. Reid makes, for me his explanation lacks the true essence of the origin of the lament. I suggest that lament begins with the realization that something "emotionally" is not right. I further propose that lament emanates from an emotional upheaval occurring within the life of the individual or community, causing a change to occur in the homeostasis of the individual or community. The fact that something is not right in and of itself does not automatically lead a person to a posture of lamenting. Therefore, my assertion is that the lament finds it origin in the emotional response of the individual or community confronted with a crisis. I believe a key to understanding the position I am proposing is in the following observation defining the word *cartharsis*.

Catharsis is derived from a Greek word meaning "to cleanse or purify" and commonly referred to as the ventilation of feelings. Catharsis generally refers to the process in which there is a sudden, overwhelming expression of emotion (e.g., crying), which results in the release of tension.[30]

For me, this definition is comprehensive enough to encompass the nature and origin of the lament. The ventilation of feelings and expression of emotions is addressed, which I believe constitute the essence of lament. Furthermore, I believe that it also captures the ideas of both lament and grief and makes a statement regarding the relatedness of the two. In embracing this understanding of grief and lament, I am suggesting that grief is a precipitator, which leads to the lament of an individual or community.

In this part of my discussion, I have sought to provide a framework on which to establish and present a basis for the use of Psalms in grief intervention. Another step necessary in establishing my position is conducting a brief examination of the Psalms, particularly the Psalms of lament to identify the grief process found therein.

Psalms of Lament

Having explored definitions of grief and lament, the attention will now shift to a study of these two subjects as presented in the book of Psalms. The Psalms contains many Scriptures revealing the numerous instances of God's people, both individual and community, lamenting, i.e., crying out to God in times of distress or trouble. The images I see in the Psalms of lament reflect a prevailing sense of loss.

Walter Brueggemann suggests three general themes or groupings of the Psalms. He divides them into Psalms of 1) Orientation, 2) Disorientation and, 3) New Orientation.[31] In organizing the Psalms in this manner, Brueggemann is suggesting a structure that exists in human life and experiences. The theme of *orientation* suggests that human life consists of seasons of goodness, satisfaction, and well-being. This concept also intimates a view of the homeostasis of individual or community life as orderly and right. Additionally, the theme suggests a time of joy and peace with life, God, and creation in which praise and thanksgiving emanate from the individual or community toward God for His blessings.

The *disorientation* theme reflects a time of personal or communal frustration, hurt, pain, and other crises resulting in the disorientation of the individual or community. I refer to disorientation as a sense of loss. My contention also is that *disorientation* refers to confusion, perplexity, or bewilderment. These feelings all suggest a condition of loss. This sense of loss leads the person into an experience of grief because of the loss encountered. At this point, the individual or community is expressing its emotions, anguish, anger, and loss of balance with life and events occurring in life. Inherent also in this phase is the longing of the heart, the search for hope, guidance for direction, and the desire to find peace.

Finally, Brueggemann suggests the theme of a *new orientation* to identify the decisive point where life takes a turn and results in resolution and regaining homeostasis. This step is a move from the problems and pains the individual has been confronting, to a newness or freshness. It is the intervention of God making all things new, giving birth to a new hope, dreams, and aspirations for living. Although Brueggemann contends that we frequently move from a settled orientation into a season of disorientation, and from disorientation to a new orientation, he is also careful to state that he is not implying a cyclical movement but rather connections that occur in life.

These Psalms give evidence of a variety of emotions that are all part of the human struggle. They express the emotions of anger, despair, hope, and joy. They also go on to raise questions of justice, vengeance, suffering, and vindication. Each individual wrestles with these issues and other issues that confront our human frailty and overall human condition. When these conditions perplex, challenge, disturb, or vex us, we lament.

In describing the structure of the book of Psalms, J. David Pleins uses three trajectories to investigate its content and form, the first of which I make mention:

> The first trajectory arises out of individual and communal suf-
> fering and addresses its speech to God. In the first part of the
> book, we hear individuals and the entire community speak
> out of their suffering and their hopes. The movement of these
> first chapters schematizes the movement of the Psalter itself,
> namely from lament to praise. In its unceasing struggle out of
> lament toward trust, thanksgiving, and ultimately praise, the
> community and the many individuals within that community
> seek to wrestle with God in their suffering, their oppression,
> their expectation, and their liberation.[32]

In this excerpt, Dr. Pleins contends that the Psalms are largely directed at the expression of human predicament and struggle. The struggle to arrive at answers or solutions later results in expressions of thanksgiving and praise to the One Who is able to sustain them and bring them through their crisis.

His second trajectory directs attention to the idea that the community's struggle does not take place in a political vacuum; therefore, questions prevail in this section. He states:

> The second section of the book is taken up with the question
> of political structures, the politics of hope, and divine gover-
> nance. Issues of war and rule are part of the divine economy,
> and the demands of God impinge on the operation of the state
> and its several institutions. Here we see the community's hopes

and tragedies are inextricably intertwined with the political structures of the day.[33]

I believe that the aim of Dr. Plenis is to assist in identifying the crises of individuals and communities, follow their course through these crises, and arrive at worship despite their current actual or perceived dangers. Furthermore, the second trajectory infers the political structures as a participant in causing the situations of grief or lament in the life of the individual or community. He is, in effect, stating that the state and its institutions, the government, and political proponents contribute to the struggles faced by individuals and community, which find their expression in laments.

Many scholars agree regarding the use of the Psalms in grief counseling because the experiences of the psalmist and his community relate to the many diverse experiences people encounter in crises. Furthermore, the process found in the Psalms addressing particular crises proved beneficial to those who found themselves involved in similar struggles or crises. These Lament Psalms are expressions from the heart of the psalmist that give examples of confronting and handling situations that led to a time of disorientation. A type of road map, providing direction to one who can lead the individual(s) out of his or her distress is in the psalmist's expressions. It is my contention that the precipitator in many of the laments is grief based on a type of loss experienced by the individual(s). The evidence of this view is in Psalm 30:7b-10:

Thou didst hide thy face, I was troubled.
[8]I cried to thee, O LORD; and unto the LORD I made supplication.
[9]What profit is there in my blood, when I go down to the pit? Shall the dust praise thee? shall it declare thy truth?
[10]Hear, O LORD, and have mercy upon me: LORD, be thou my helper.

In this Psalm, I believe that the psalmist laments the loss of divine presence. He struggles with God Who seems absent from the presence of the individual. The psalmist is unable at this point in his struggle to experience the presence of the Almighty. The psalmist begins this Psalm with expressions of joy and praise for the goodness of God, which is a sense of *orientation*, as Brueggemann suggests.

The focus of verse 7 evidences the psalmist's expression shifting from *orientation* to *disorientation*. This seemingly sudden transition gives no indication of a particular crisis issue arising. The only precipitator appearing in the verses given is the absence or loss of the presence of God, which also hastened self-examination by the psalmist regarding his own life.

Ultimately, the psalm ends with a note of affirmation and celebration of the goodness of God through the period of disorientation resulting in a *new orientation*. This psalm reflects a form found in many of the psalms of lament. However, a repeat of the pattern is not a reoccurring phenomenon found in the same order. The presence of these phases implies a process of grief that manifests itself in these forms of the psalms.

Regarding the issue of the form of the Psalms, Walter Brueggemann references the work of Claus Westermann. In summarizing Westermann's work regarding the form in Psalms of lament, Brueggemann suggests that the movement of these Psalms unite under two discernable parts: 1) Plea, and 2) Praise.[34] Westermann says,

> The following are constituent parts of the lament of the individual: address, lament, confession of trust, or assurance of being heard, petition, vow to praise. This is the basic scheme, but it never becomes stereotyped. The possibilities of variation are unusually numerous.[35]

On this same subject, Donald Capps says the following regarding the form or structure of the lament: "The psalms of lament have a characteristic form that allows an unlimited number of variations but requires a fixed sequence of elements."[36]

Following this statement regarding form, Capps references the work of Bernhard W. Anderson, who identifies six elements that exist in this form as follows:

1) **Address** to God, a brief cry for help
2) **Complaint**, expression of one's complaint or problem
3) **Confession of Trust**, expression of confidence in God in spite of one's current difficulties
4) **Petition**, specific appeals to God for intervention and deliverance
5) **Words of Assurance**, certainty that the psalmist petition will be heard
6) **Vow to Praise**, vow to testify to the name of God for what has been done in the supplicant's behalf[37]

Anderson's six elements correspond to the eight parts of the lament psalms identified by Claus Westermann as follows:

1) Address, with an introductory cry for help and or turning to God
2) Lament
3) Confession of Trust
4) Petition: for God to be favorable, for God to intervene
5) Assurance of being heard
6) Double wish, petition for God to intervene
7) Vow to praise
8) Praise of God, only where petition has been answered[38]

There is consistency in the emphasis of the lament psalms. Furthermore, although most scholars may present a varying structure or form, the basic process is the same, suggesting a process or patterns of emotional development that occur within individuals when confronted with crises. In particular is this pattern true in the crisis of grief or loss. I perceive in each of the psalms of lament a struggle on the part of the individual or community to address personal or communal loss.

As stated in the introduction of this work, my purpose aims at examining the use of the Psalms in grief situations. By defining grief and lament and exploring lament found in the psalms, my conclusion is that the primary purpose of the lament psalms is focused upon the individual's or communities' grief. I contend that the precipitator of the laments is grief or a sense of loss. The expressions of a community of people or an individual whose life structure has been disrupted are seen in these psalms. These expressions of individuals and community prove beneficial in caring for and assisting people in crises today. One example of an individual using this form of literature to respond to crisis in her own life is writer, speaker, and liturgist, Ann Weems.

In her book titled *Psalms of Lament*, Weems becomes the psalmist and gives expressions of the deep emotions that flow within planted by grief in her life. Weems, encouraged by Bruggemann to write her expressions, says the following:

> I know my psalms are not finished. Anger and alleluias careen around within me, sometimes colliding. Lamenting and laughter sit side by side in a heart that yearns for the peace that passes all understanding. Those who believe in the midst of their weeping will know where I stand.[39]

THE RELATIONSHIP OF THE PSALMS
TO AFRICAN AMERICAN SPIRITUALS
AND HYMNS

This analysis of the Psalms and their relationship to the African American spirituals and hymns will not focus on the entire 150 Psalms; rather, its focus relates primarily to the psalms of individual or communal lament. To clarify my approach, I am defining relationships as the connection or points of similarity or the inter-relatedness existing between these music genres. Reference to hymns in this assessment will appear inconspicuous because much of the information given regarding the African American spirituals is also true of African American hymns. Therefore, as I refer to the spirituals, I am also referring to the hymns except when noted. As already stated, my contention is that the psalms of lament represent the recorded expressions of an individual or community in dealing with their respective crises.

Each of the lament psalms derives from the life of the individual or community and is not a fabricated or unreal crisis. The crisis is real to the psalmist whether perceived or present. Hence, the crisis is a part of the overall scheme of life for everyone. The lament psalms proceed to tell the story of the individual or community as they encounter their crises. This aspect of the lament psalm is also comparable to the development of the spirituals and hymns of the African American community. The same manner in which the lament psalms are expressions

---

49

of the individual or community, so are the spirituals and hymns of the African American church. I believe it is conceivable that the spirituals of the African American people are the lament psalms of that community. This idea appears to be conveyed by George A. Lindbeck as he discusses his cultural-linguistic view. In his discussion of religion and experience he states, "The linguistic-cultural model is part of an outlook that stresses the degree to which human experience is shaped, molded, and in a sense constituted by cultural and linguistic forms."[40]

Thus, the linguistic forms of the psalms, spirituals, and hymns reflect the experiences of the people who sang, wrote, or otherwise expressed the struggles and plight of their own existence. The spirituals of the African slaves are more than simply folk songs, moans, or sorrow songs; they represent the struggle of the slaves to make sense of the crisis that entered their lives and disrupted the homeostasis of that community.

Viewing the psalms, spirituals, and hymns as expressive components of life suggests a linking of the expressions of life with the life of the individual who experiences life. They are the expressions from the lives of individuals and communities, their stories. These stories express the struggles, pains, sorrows, joys, grief, and laments of the individual(s) and their community. Ann Wimberly, Assistant Professor of Christian Education and Church Music at the Interdenominational Theological Center in Atlanta, Georgia, makes a significant observation about the story-linking process which, I believe, serves to support my position. She states the following:

> Story-linking is a process whereby we connect parts of our everyday stories with the Christian faith story in the Bible and the lives of exemplars of the Christian faith outside the Bible. In this process, we link with Bible stories by using them as

mirrors through which we reflect critically on the liberation we have already found or are still seeking. We also link with our Christian faith heritage by learning about exemplars who chose a way of living based on their understanding of liberation and vocation found in scripture. By linking with Christian faith heritage stories, we may be encouraged and inspired by predecessors who have faced life circumstances with which we readily identify.[41]

Although this work by Ann Wimberly focuses upon Christian Education in the African American church and community, the principle of her position is valid relative to the meaning and relationship of the psalms to spirituals and hymns. Her research further suggests that the process or relationship is also educational for the community. The psalms, spirituals, and hymns not only serve as poetry and song, but they are curriculum for life, giving instruction to people in crisis-seeking solution and liberation.

Glen R. Hufnagel suggests that the relationship between the psalms and the spirituals is, in fact, an intimate relationship which has always existed. He expresses this view in the statements that follow. In these statements, Hufnagel introduces six ideas that argue the relationship or connection that exists between the psalms and spirituals. I will identify and discuss the assertions made by Hufnagel regarding the relationship between the psalms and spirituals. He begins by stating the following:

1) The 150 psalms and the entire corpus of spirituals express the same ideas and moods.[42]

In this statement, I believe Hufnagel is suggesting that the thematic emphasis of the psalms and spirituals is comparable. They are expressing ideas about the praise and worship of God as well as giving credence to the personality and circumstance of the writer. If I understand correctly, Hufnagel's use of the phrase "ideas and moods" to mean the thoughts of the people and the condition or attitude existing regarding their situation, this assertion clearly grasps the general position of the two. The theme of deliverance from oppression and liberation are definite elements or "ideas" of the lament psalms and the spirituals. Furthermore, an attitude or a "mood" of hope and anticipation of deliverance is also characteristic of the two.

2) The composers of the psalms and spirituals created their music specifically for religious worship, which explains why both genres are of the exhortative and edifying.[43]

While I agree that both genres are exhortative and edifying, I am of the position that both genres were not solely created for worship. James Cone writes:

Theologically, there is more to be said about the music of black people than what was revealed in the black spirituals. To be sure, a significant number of black people were confident that the God of Israel was involved in black history, liberating them from slavery and oppression. But not all blacks could accept the divine promises of the Bible as a satisfactory answer to the contradictions of black existence. They refused to adopt a God-centered perspective as the solution to the problem of black suffering.[44]

This view gave rise to a worldly dimension of the spirituals, producing a genre of music referred to as "The Blues." Cone further suggests: "The blues tell about the strength of black people to survive, to endure, and to shape existence while living in the midst of oppressive contradictions."[45]

The Blues represent a secular form of spirituals. Many of the spirituals served as field songs used to make the work go faster or to encourage one another to complete the work ahead. My contention is that they were not all specifically aimed at worship. Hildred Roach sheds light on this matter also, pointing out:

> Despite the overabundance of Biblical words used in the majority of the spirituals, their functions were not purely religious. They were constantly used in the search for freedom, in religious services, to teach, gossip, scold, signal, or to delight in the telling of tales. They also relieved the minds and bodies of the enslaved and they served more significantly as a means of informing the slaves of their own affairs, i.e., social politics, deliverance, escape, or satire.[46]

Although these songs do possess exhortations, some of the exhortative expressions are self-directed as well as others that emphasize the praise and worship of God. Many of these songs possessed double and triple meanings, speaking through coded messages regarding their existence in this world and otherworldly directed.

The Psalms of Lament appear to have this similar thrust. The psalmist directs the readers and hearers of the lament to praise and worship God but also openly expresses emotions and feelings. These expressions reveal times of discouragement and even surrender to the crisis that did not foster an attitude of worship. However, despite this absence, I agree that the components of edification and exhortation are present in both the psalms of lament and the spirituals.

3) Both psalms and spirituals do more than document biblical history as told in many of the Old Testament narratives; they also capture the worldview of those who created the music, including how they perceived such things as life and death.[47]

Hufnagel makes a very significant observation. The Psalms and the spirituals express more than a biblical story; they also reveal political, economic, ethical, racial, and societal issues confronting the people of that day and time. The hymns in this case are not as similar in their expressions. The expressions made by the authors of the psalms and spirituals often very clearly and at other times imply the overall view of the writer regarding life situations and their effect on the people.

4) The symbolism in both the psalms and spirituals is sufficiently broad to make their messages in today's liturgy about as meaningful to the contemporary worshiper as to the original creators.[48]

The symbolism used in the psalms and spirituals make the messages transferable to many contemporary situations and settings. This imagery also gives way to multiple meanings and interpretations of the text of the psalm or spiritual. Hufnagel's assertion points to another significant similarity in the psalms and spirituals; that is, the sometimes misinterpretation or improper meanings given which do an injustice to the work of the writer.

Hymns of the African American church also contain much symbolism, which sometimes offers a promising view of life that cannot be delivered. However, most of the psalms and spirituals receive proper interpretation. Furthermore, I believe that the symbolism used in the psalms and spirituals make them meaningful and effective to people as helpful instruments in times of crisis.

5) In terms of literary form, the psalms, like the spirituals, employ parallel syntax, refrain, recapitulation, repetition, and strophic and responsorial form.[49]

The language of the lament psalms and spirituals also make them effective. They both syntactically offer expressions that are relative to the hearers and individuals experiencing similar crises. The form follows the struggle of the individual. Although the orderly flow may differ, the process is the same. As literary works, the spirituals are a form of psalms, and the psalms are a form of spirituals. They are both literary expressions of communities and individuals confronting and addressing their crises.

> 6) Perhaps the most striking similarity exist specifically between the psalm "lament" and the spiritual "sorrow song": both commence with an individual or community cry for help to overcome sorrow, oppression, or transgression, and conclude faithfully and joyfully on a high pitch of praise.[50]

This view agrees with the position of Brueggemann, Capps, Westermann, and others who cite the flow of the lament psalms. I believe this pattern exists because the expressions reveal the heart and the emotions of the community or individual experiencing the crisis.

In conclusion, these statements made by Hufnagel voice the views that I also hold. He sets forth a position regarding the psalms and spirituals that I believe are clear and well developed. This analysis may miss other significant connections between the psalms and spirituals; however, I believe that this view summarizes the truth concerning both literary or musical forms. I add to this that because of the hymns' origin and original intent, they are not as parallel to the psalms and spirituals in their original forms. However, many of the original hymns, which were later arranged by African American songwriters, possess the ideas like the psalms and spirituals. They too present struggle, crisis, lament, and hope. This relationship as discussed here exposes the nature of psalms, spirituals, and hymns, and their use in the community and life of individuals dealing with various crises.

THE USE OF PSALMS, SPIRITUALS, AND HYMNS AS GRIEF INTERVENTION TOOLS

THE PSALMS AS GRIEF INTERVENTION TOOLS

Of the many texts of Scripture used in grief situations, most counselors and caregivers use the lament psalms more than any other collection of writings. In a variety of ways, the lament psalms are useful as resources in grief intervention. Donald Capps addresses the use of the psalms in grief counseling situations by pastoral counselors Wayne Oates, Seward Hiltner, and Carroll Wise, expressing the major reason he believes these psalms are beneficial in this manner:

> A major reason for their emphasis on the psalms is the psalms' reflection of human emotional experience, and for these authors, pastoral counseling aims to help counselees express and clarify their feelings. By "feelings" they do not mean emotions that come and go, but deep feelings that reflect serious intrapsychic conflicts.[51]

Each of these authors shares the belief in the efficacy of the psalms in grief counseling because they too reflect the deep emotional experiences of the psalmist. This fact alone gives the psalms a reality perspective that individuals experiencing crisis are most often readily able to identify. The focus of each of these counselors is upon the inner struggles, feelings, or reactions of the individual in crisis. Capps suggests that the use of the psalms of lament is effective in moving the individual experiencing grief or loss through the stages of grief already identified. He further gives three reasons for his position regarding the effectiveness of the psalms of lament in counseling, stating,

> In the first place, the lament can help define the basic objectives of grief…The ultimate objectives of grief counseling are grounded in the assurance that the counselee's suffering and petitions are shared by others. In the second place, the psalm of lament clarifies the relationship between counselor and counselee in grief counseling. As a mediator between the sufferer and God, the counselor accepts the counselee's negative self-justifying feelings, shares and clarifies the counselor's petitions, and helps the counselee give concrete expression to his or her praise of God. In the third place, the psalms of lament reflect the sense in which grief counseling involves a non-directive method. Like many psalms, the grief counseling process is not rigid or forced. Because it has emotional components similar to those of laments, it facilitates the intervention of God. It the psalmist's experience of God is reflected in the abrupt shifts that occur in the lament, grief counseling should be no less open and adaptable to similar abrupt shifts and experiences of intervention.[52]

These comments by Capps summarize the use of the psalms of lament in grief counseling and are helpful expressions of my thoughts regarding their use. They suggest that his use of the psalms and perhaps the use of the psalms by others are specifically related to having a body of literature which serves to open the individual by relating to the experiences of another. In this manner, the psalms prove helpful and beneficial to individuals seeking ways to express or give vent to the crisis they are experiencing.

THE SPIRITUALS AS GRIEF INTERVENTION TOOLS

Historically, little or no formal research has been conducted on the use of spirituals as grief intervention tools. A study of sufferings and experiences of African slaves are the primary source of use in providing information regarding this subject. To my knowledge, no definitive work exists about African American spirituals and grief. However, many inferences can be found in diverse writings on the subject of music, or music in the African American church.

Because the African slaves arriving in the New World disconnected from their home and community, they developed ways to cope with their situation. From the time of their capture to their arrival in a new place, the slaves experienced grief repeatedly and were without freedom to express the grief they felt. Their captors could hear much of the outward expressions of their grief such as crying and moans, but the slaves encountered many barriers that resulted in other situations of grief within the individuals. The losses experienced by the slaves were numerous. The loss of community, freedom, communal language, lineage, traditions, and more left the African slaves bereft of their humanity and dignity. Theirs was the epitome of grief. Encumbered with the weight of grief and loss, the slave community sought and developed coping mechanisms to deal with their struggle, grief, and losses.

As is stated of the psalms being expressions of the inner thoughts and feelings of the individual, the spirituals developed as expressions of the same nature for the slaves. The spirituals functioned as a means of addressing the pain, injustice, grief, and losses encountered by the slaves. Just as the lament psalms emerged as expressions of the human soul, the spirituals also express the cries from the souls of the African American slave.

The slaves had no counselors skilled in using the spirituals as therapeutic instruments; rather, they were laments easily identified with by those who were familiar with the pain. When the slaves began to hear the stories of the Bible and related to the oppressed people found in the writings of Scripture, they were able to relate in crisis to the people of God who suffered. In this process, many of the stories of Scripture commingled with the spirituals. In this manner, a method of addressing the pain, grief, and sorrow of individuals and community developed. The spirituals did not solve, they soothed; they did not replace, they restored; they did not change, they comforted. The spirituals spoke to the inner pains and grief of people seeking to survive a crisis.

HYMNS AS GRIEF INTERVENTION TOOLS

The use of hymns as intervention tools primarily address the comfort of the individual and the eventual expressions of praise and glory to God. The hymns were reminders of the sovereignty of God, the omnipotence of God, and the providential care of God for His people. In the African American community, these hymns, as rearrangements of earlier hymns, took on a structure and form like the spirituals, but with a stronger slant toward the celebration and shout of the victory over the crisis.

Most counselors appear to use hymns as consolation tools. In this manner the hymns tend only to console and may not lead to praise. In the African American church, the consolation leads to the affirmation of God's ultimate goodness regardless of the crisis. Consequently, the counselee is invited to release the tension of worry, anger, fear, doubt, depression, and guilt and give God the glory.

Some advocates suggest that this idea is in no way beneficial to the individual(s) encountering crisis because the person's feelings are only masked, and their deep feelings within are not addressed. Others argue to the contrary, taking the position that the deep feelings of the individual are expressed in the determination of the individual to shout, rejoice, weep, and praise God with their pain. This method does not ignore the crisis. On the contrary, this method sees the crisis as a circumstance that a person "goes through"—not "remains in."

In this analysis I have sought to look at and discuss the relationship of the Psalms to spirituals and hymns in grief intervention. The aim was to assess their role in the grief process and their historical use in the lives of individuals and communities. The meanings of grief and lament have been examined to understand the perspectives of each and observed their relationship with the psalms of lament. Furthermore, the relationship existing between the psalms of lament with the African American spirituals and hymns has been evaluated and their similarities addressed. Lastly, having suggested the previous uses of these three literary forms regarding grief intervention, my aim now is to develop these ideas into a paradigm of ministry, i.e., using these resources in this present day as tools in grief intervention.

SPIRITUALS AND HYMNS AS PASTORAL CARE TOOLS IN CRISIS INTERVENTION

In this study, I shall focus on the practical usage of African American spirituals and hymns, giving particular attention to their utilization as tools of pastoral care in crisis intervention. My argument on this subject will unfold in the following manner. First, I suggest definitions of crisis to give a view of the overall scope of this work. Secondly, I present a review of the uses of these genres with a discussion of responses given from a questionnaire completed by members of the church where I serve as pastor. Finally, I shall present my view of how spirituals and hymns are useful in pastoral care as crisis intervention tools and suggest a possible model for using spirituals and hymns in grief crisis intervention.

DEFINING CRISIS

To be alive and to be human is to know crisis. No one is immune. Whether through serious illness, the death of a loved one, loss of a job, serious accident, or some other traumatic experience, we all realize sooner or later that we are not invulnerable, that "accidents" don't just happen to the other guy. Somewhere, sometime, in some way you will face a crisis.[53]

Crisis is an inevitable experience everyone will face at one time or another at various stages of life. To construct a view of the meaning of crisis in this analysis, of necessity, some definitions of crisis must be addressed. The following are definitions of the word *crisis*:

> The Chinese picture symbol for the word *crisis* indicates both danger and opportunity, the danger of loss and hurt and the opportunity for gain and health.[54]

> A *crisis* can be understood as a crucial time and turning point. It is the term for an individual's internal reaction to an external hazard. It involves a temporary loss of coping abilities, a paralysis of action. Any definition of crisis makes a tacit assumption that the emotional dysfunction is reversible.[55]

> *Crisis* is an upset in the emotional steady state of an individual or social unit caused by events which overwhelm pre-existing mechanisms for maintaining psychological equilibrium.[56]

These definitions serve to suggest that crisis is the response of the individual or community to an event or situation which prompts a type of action from the person(s) encountering the event. The event itself is not the crisis; the crisis is the resulting state of the individual(s). Life consists of a multitude of events that affect the balance of an individual's life. These events vary, ranging from one extreme to another.

In this work, the event is loss. Throughout this analyzation, the event of loss stands as the issue and its effect on the individual(s) experiencing the loss. Another view of this idea reveals the event as the precipitator causing the person to enter a state of crisis. In his book *Crisis Counseling*, Howard Stone states: "An outside precipitator or emotional hazard, such as death, divorce, or job loss, usually triggers crisis; these precipitators are always situational and frequently inter-personal in nature."[57]

Stone also suggests that in crisis intervention giving attention to the precipitator, the cause of the crisis, is important. Consequently, the individual(s) in crisis and the intervener is adequately informed and able to determine the proper methods of intervention. Stone says that individuals experience crises when loss is perceived or threatened.

> The loss can be of a significant person, a love or dependency relationship, financial support, health, life, a family role a sense of worthfulness, values, or meaning of life. Losses do not necessarily occur only in the form of divorce or death.[58]

Based upon the research I have done, the conclusion I came to may seem radical or totally inept; however, I must submit that slavery is an event that existed before the enslavement of Africans by Europeans and others. Scripture records the fact that slavery existed. However, in the African culture, slavery was not a dehumanization of the individual; rather, its methodology involved the resolution of debts owed to another. The fulfillment of the debt through servitude and the eventual release of the debt or obligation obtained the freedom of the individual. Therefore, slavery as a means of repaying a debt was not a new experience.

As slavery took the form for dehumanization, oppression, and disrespect for a race of people, the event of slavery caused a new response to an existing practice. The event is not the crisis; rather, the crisis represents the losses experienced by the individual(s) because of the way this form of slavery destroyed relationships, dehumanized a race of people, and removed them from their home.

Slavery represents the overwhelming losses experienced by individuals and a community. Perhaps this view of the events that shaped life for African Americans gave rise to an eschatology fostering a view that events come and go but can be endured if one has the proper perspective of life. I believe the losses in life precipitate the crisis of grief. At the point of wrestling with the grief crisis, individuals who are experiencing emotions, frustrations, despair, etc., seek to find coping mechanisms for their grief. The preceding definitions and views give meaning to my position.

Having briefly considered definitions of the word crisis, a review of the use of these genres obtained from a questionnaire administered to the congregation where I serve as pastor will be shared.

THE USE OF SPIRITUALS AND HYMNS

As stated in an previous essay, the spirituals and hymns of the African American Church possess a certain quality and meaning within the African American Community which has allowed them to serve the community in a multifarious manner. Historical evidence reveals that these spirituals and hymns contained coded messages and multiple meanings regarding life and death, slavery and freedom, joy and suffering. Because of the many interpretations possible for these songs, they were also invaluable to the African American community in handling crisis, loss, and grief situations. The losses encountered by African Americans through the years led them to seek an appropriate means to address the conditions they were experiencing. The result was a familiar vehicle used by Africans in the past.

As a response to a new crisis, songs deeply inculcated within their being were born as a new genre called "spirituals." These songs contained a language that was familiar to the oppressed and served as a meaningful method of handling the crisis they now face. Language has always been a significant part of the African American experience.

Since the days of slavery, African slaves developed and employed a language that their masters and his cohorts were incapable of understanding. This language was often filled with imagery, analogies, metaphors, and symbolism related to a common experience of those who spoke it. This language related to the struggles and agonies of the slaves and often revealed an eschatological hope that enabled them to endure. Their language intertwined with their belief and understanding of God and Jesus. In his book entitled *Shoes That Fit Our Feet*, Dwight N. Hopkins makes the following statement:

> An examination of slaves' lives and thought about God conveys several important factors in the lineage of the black church. For instance, slave theology consistently experienced God dwelling with those in bondage, personal and systemic. The black religious experience prevented any separation between the sacred and the secular, the church and the community...Moreover, the slaves distinguished their humanity from the white slave master. For blacks, God and Jesus called them to use all means possible to pursue religiously a human status of equality.[59]

This explanation suggests that the African slaves incorporated their experiences into a theology of the sovereignty of God and developed a language of inspiration, hope, and survival that was expressed in their music. They did not seek to separate God from their experiences but viewed God as being consciously aware of their plight and on the side of the oppressed. Thus, the language used by slaves in their songs and everyday conversations spoke of joy and equality that transcended their current circumstances. During their struggle and oppression, the church stood as a symbol of hope.

Though slaves did not have direct access to the specifics of their former African religious practices and beliefs, they did maintain some theological remnants—religious Africanism. Unfortunately, the European slave trade, the practice of mixing Africans from different villages, white people's prohibition of the use of African languages, and the fading memories of succeeding slave progeny all served to dampen the vibrancy of a systematic African theology in slave thought. Nevertheless, enslaved Africans brought religious ideas and forces of theological habit with them to the so-called New World.[60]

The slaves maintained a strong sense of family and community even through the tragic defilement and separation of family units. A connection remained between the individual and the community. This connection transcended status, location, and situation, and ran through the African church and its community. This link also exists in the language of the songs of disenfranchised people.

African religions gave rise to a dynamic interplay between community and individual. Whatever happened to the communal gathering affected the individual; whatever happened to the individual had an impact on the community. Such a theological view of humanity cuts across bourgeois notions of white Christianity's individualism and "me-first-isms." It seeks to forge a group solidarity and identity, beginning with God, proceeding through the ancestors to the community and immediate family, and continuing even to the unborn. One cannot be a human being unless one becomes a part of, feels a responsibility to, and serves the community. To preserve the community's well being (through liberation) in African religions is to preserve the individual's well being (through salvation). Thus, salvation and liberation become a holistic individual-collective and personal-systemic ultimate concern.[61]

The preceding view as expressed by Dwight Hopkins discloses what I identify as the nucleus for the development of a language for the African community that expresses the ultimate concerns of the individual and community, shapes the manner in which communication develops, and identifies the doctrine of the people as they exist in community. Hopkins' statement also suggests that there is a doctrinal substructure to the relationship existing in the African community. This substructure leads to forms of expression.

The conditions of slavery in the United States made it often impossible or imprudent for African slaves to speak directly of their hopes. They were compelled to find a language that would unmistakably express their hopes for a reversal in their fortunes and at the same time conceal that message from the slave-owners. The apocalyptic language found in the Bible was a ready vehicle. Its striking and colorful images of a radically different future, while rejected by most post-Enlightenment Christian communities, were the cornerstone of African American public Christian discourse. Talk of rapture, heaven, pearly gates, and winged saints fills African American folklore and still heavily influences preaching in some African American churches. There are at least three reasons that apocalyptic language suited the purposes of newly converted African Christians in slavery. First, this language reflected an ancient cosmology that put God firmly in charge of the universe. Second, it was consistent with the political interest of the oppressed people whom God promised to deliver. Third, this language was the expressive vehicle for the imagination of people convinced of their future liberation. This language did more; however, than simply describe the future it told a story. The story of God's rectification of the world called its hearers into a creative participation in the promised salvation... Apocalyptic language contained intimations of a new order and a new reality that spoke to the deepest yearning of a dislocated and estranged people.[62]

This language along with the expressions of other biblical stories, including the psalms of lament, were influential in shaping and giving meaning to the spirituals as a new form of expression. The following is an example of this language and meaning as shown in the song "All God's Chillun." The song finds its basis in the following passages of Scripture:

- *"He hath put a new song in my mouth"* (Psalm 40:3).
- *"God...who giveth songs in the night"* (Job 35:10b)
- *"I call to remembrance my song in the night"* (Psalm 77:6a)
- *"And they sung as it were new songs before the throne"* (Revelation 14:13a)
- *"And white robes were given unto every one of them"* (Revelation 6:11a)

Hear the slaves as they offered assurance and hope to each other amid their crisis:

I got a song, you got a song,
All God's chillun got a song;
When we get to heab'n, goin' sing a new song,
Goin' sing all over God's heab'n.

I got shoes, you got shoes,
All God's chillun got shoes;
When we get to heab'n, goin' put on my shoes,
Goin' walk all over God's heab'n.

One can hear in the slave songs the mourning and groaning of an oppress people, and yet one can recognize in them also the hopes, yearnings, and determination of invincible spirits.[63]

Another spiritual expressing the deep emotions of slaves to survive, despite their hostile and dehumanizing environment and put their losses and pains in perspective, is the spiritual titled, "I've Been 'Buked and I've been Scorn." The psalm of lament identified with this spiritual is Psalm 44:13-16, which says,

> *"Thou makest us a reproach to our neighbors, a scorn and a derision to them that are round about us. Thou makest us a byword among the heathen, a shaking of the head among the people. My confusion is continually before me, and the shame of my face covered me, for the voice of him that reproacheth and blasphemeth; by reason of the enemy and avenger."*

The lyrics of the song are as follows:

> *I've been 'buked and I've been scorned,*
> *I've been 'buked and I've been scorned,*
> *I've been talked about, sho'as you're born.*
>
> *Dere is trouble all over dis world,*
> *Dere is trouble all over dis world,*
> *Children, dere is trouble all over dis world.*
>
> *I ain't gwine to lay my 'ligion down,*
> *I ain't gwine to lay my 'ligion down,*
> *Children, I ain't gwine lay to my 'ligion down,*

This song and others like it express the despair and devastating feelings of slavery upon the individual. They reveal the abuse, disregard, and the disdain of the slave. However, the song concludes with a vow to maintain and progress. A vow to continue to trust the God of the oppressed, unwilling to lay down their faith and hope that God will come through on their behalf, Delores Williams quotes historian John Blassingame who states,

> Convinced that God watches over him, the slave bore his and her earthly afflictions, in order to earn a heavenly reward. Often he disobeyed his earthly master's rules to keep his heavenly master's commandments.... Religious faith gave an ultimate purpose to his life, a sense of communal fellowship and personal worth.... In short, religion helped him preserve his mental health. Trust in God was conducive to psychic health insofar that it excluded all anxiety-producing preoccupation by recognition of a loving providence.[64]

These words speak of a certain innate sense of God's providential care and His sovereign hand upon the life of the slave. This view encourages the eschatology of hope. When slavery and oppression dehumanized the slaves and discrimination and segregation degraded them, the black church taught them to sing:

> *We are our heavenly father's children.*
> *And we all know that he loves us, one and all.*

When the male slaves were weak physically and spiritually, and female slaves were robbed of hope, the language of the spirituals and the unlearned black preacher pushed them on, encouraging them through song: *Walk together, children; don't get weary!*

When death invaded the life of the slaves, the message of the spirituals told the slaves that over yonder they would:

> *Sit at the welcome table,*

eat and never get hungry,
drink and never get thirsty.

The African American spirituals declared a language of assurance. When illness would wear down the strength of the slave and slave mothers had again seen their child taken from them, a message of consolation from the spiritual came in song:

Soon ah will be done, with the trouble of the world.

Along with this assurance, a language of celebration rang out when they considered no longer having to deal with the white slave master. Although he was a church-going person, the reason for their celebration was in knowing that not all who entered the church's doors went to heaven.

Everybody talkin' bout Heaven that ain't goin there...

The songs, the preaching, and the testifying in the black church had a significant role in developing and perpetuating a language of hope in the community. It is increasingly clear that the language of the African slaves proved vital to their survival and continued existence. Their language was not only a system of words for conversation, but vitally represented expressions of a people who created a oneness in and among those who spoke this language. Regardless of the age or gender of the individual, the proper language made whatever the situation or experience one that could give birth to hope.

Despite the obvious disadvantage of not having the freedom to express and share with others, spirituals became the vehicle by which situations and circumstances became transformed. The language of the spirituals broke down barriers, gave them an upper hand in their oppression, and created an eschatology inextricably connected to the slave's experiences. Regarding eschatology James Evans states,

Eschatology in black theology is inseparable from the struggle of African Americans for freedom. As one theologian puts it, "The whole of Black eschatology could be summed up in one word: liberation. Black theologians proclaim that God is the Liberator who acts in history to set people free from whatever keeps them in bondage to a life which is less than human." It is impossible to understand fully the significance of eschatology in African American religious experience without attention to its role in the freedom struggle of black people. Eschatology refers to the consummation and rectification of history and the persistence of hope. The vision of a new order was indispensable to Africans languishing in the foul embrace of slavery because it kept the fires of freedom burning in their hearts. Yet, they were not content to claim solely an inner freedom. The idea of the reign of God or the Promised Land compelled them to proclaim and approximate it in their individual and collective existence.[65]

Eschatology permeated the language and therefore the music of the slaves that could not be separated from their experiences. The language and song of the slave, the experiences of slavery and eschatology are inextricably connected. This relationship is manifested in the multiplicity of ways that the slaves expressed their eschatology. It existed in the sermons preached, the spirituals, hymns, and other music sung, as well as the everyday conversation of the slaves with one another. If conversation was not possible, expression was found in the spirituals and other songs sung in the fields while the slave worked. This eschatology served as the basis for the slave's reason to keep the faith and never give up the fight. This eschatological language in their songs is the foundation of their transferred hope.

I have included only a small representation of the many spirituals instrumental in engendering hope in the lives of the African Americans slaves and the generations that followed. Dr. Wyatt Tee Walker suggests, "If you listen to what Black people are singing religiously, it is a clue to what is happening to them sociologically."[66]

Dr. Walker's statement provides insight into the music and meanings of the music in the African American community, even discussing the Depression era and its effect on African Americans. He describes the situation as a bad time in which the African American community was falling apart. However, he recalls, during this time Thomas Dorsey lifted the hopes of the Black people by designing a hymn of trust and hope. The words of this hymn encouraged hope in the midst of a pressure-cooker crisis.

The Lord Will Make a Way Somehow

Like a ship that's tossed and driven,
Battered by an angry sea.
When the storms of life are raging,
And their fury falls on me.
I wonder what I have done,
That makes this race so hard to run.
Then I say to my soul, "Take courage!"
The Lord will make a way somehow.

Chorus:
The Lord will make a way somehow,
When beneath the cross I bow.
He will take away each sorrow,
Let Him have your burden now.
When the load bears down so heavy,
The weight is shown upon my brow.

There's a sweet relief in knowing,
The Lord will make a way somehow.

⌒

The hymns like the spirituals express an existential faith held by the African American church and community. Regardless of the crisis, their faith says God is still in control and will work things out for the good of His children.

In a questionnaire given to the congregation where I serve, many of the parishioners expressed the varied ways that the spirituals, hymns, and gospels ministered to them in their crisis. The design of the questionnaire focused on assessing the use of spirituals and hymns by individuals as a means of helping individuals cope with, weather, or survive crisis in their lives. The results indicate a great number of people who still rely on the messages of music to comfort, soothe, and strengthen them in times of crisis regardless of the precipitator.

In the responses given, an element of loss seemed to be contained in each of the crises experienced. The crises identified on the questionnaire ranged from losses through death to loss of transportation. The participants agreed that certain spirituals, hymns, and gospels proved effective in moving them through their loss. These songs, to which they refer, give direction and lead them to a new orientation and commitment to trust God.

The questionnaire was instrumental in guiding participants to revisit their crisis and share afresh how they "made it over." These responses indicate that many or most of these individuals received no formalized therapy or counseling for their depression, anxiety, or grief; yet there is indication that the ministry of the Word of God and the vehicle of music offered support and help.

I must also add here that some suggest the individuals using this method of handling their crisis did not really address their pain or loss.

Instead, they insist that the individuals simply concealed their pain or loss behind songs that made unrealistic promises. Furthermore, they infer that this process is not logical and does not make sense. However, I believe this is the essence of faith and hope. Faith really does not make sense, and, in most if not all cases, certainly is not logical. The fact that these genres of music are expressions of the soul and feelings of individuals make them applicable to many of life's situations and circumstances. This fact, therefore, makes them meaningful expressions in the lives of those who sing these songs. This finding also leads me to the position that spirituals and hymns are viable tools of pastoral care in crisis intervention. At this point, I present a model using these musical genres as tools of pastoral care in crisis intervention.

A Model for Using
Spirituals and Hymns
As Crisis Intervention Tools
in Pastoral Care

In defining pastoral care, most scholars concur that pastoral care is ministering to meet the comprehensive needs of the individual. Donald McKim suggests in the *Westminster Dictionary of Theological Terms* that *Pastoral Care* is:

> The practical expression of the church's ministry of love for the needs of the community, the people of God, and individuals. It is enacted in a wide variety of ways and through many forms of ministry.[67]

In this definition, McKim emphasizes the idea of practicality to the act of pastoral care. This emphasis lends itself to the idea that pastoral care is not merely a theoretical approach to ministering to people; rather, it is simple action in daily practical ways. Pastoral care, as this definition implies, is a verb, existing only as the people within the community of faith demonstrate it by their actions toward one another in the community.

Most definitions of pastoral care derive from the four functions of pastoral care—healing, sustaining, guiding, and reconciling[68]—as described by William A. Clebsch and Charles R. Jaekle. The following discussion is a summary of the meaning of pastoral care as presented by Clebsch and Jaekle including quotations from Ed Wimberly. The information shared from Ed Wimberly addresses the four functions of pastoral care with emphasis on the African American context. In addition to the comments of these authors, I am also including an analysis of the ways these authors address the historical implementation of these functions. I include this information to set forth this model for implementing pastoral care using spirituals and hymns, which I will also present.

THE FOUR FUNCTIONS OF PASTORAL CARE AND WAYS HISTORICALLY IMPLEMENTED

Function: HEALING

Definition:
- The pastoral function that "aims to overcome some impairment by *restoring a person to wholeness* and by leading him to advance beyond his previous condition."[69]
- Binding up the wounds, repairing the damage that has been done as a result of disease, infection, or invasion; and restoring of a condition that has been lost.[70]

Ways Historically Implemented:
- Historically, the function of healing has been carried out through such acts as anointing, exorcism, prayers to the saints, pilgrimages to shrines, charismatic healing, magic and magic medicine.[71]

Function: SUSTAINING

Definition
- The function that helps individuals endure and rise above situa-

tions in which a restoration to their previous condition is unlikely.[72]

► Helping people courageously and creatively endure and transcend difficult situations while preventing or lessening the impact of the situation; sustaining is offered when healing is not possible.[73]

Ways Historically Implemented:

► Church history records perseverance, consolation, and visitation of the sick and shut-ins as ways in which this function has been exercised.[74]

► Bringing to bear upon the person in crisis the total caring resources of the church in such a way that the person is enabled to transcend and endure circumstances that are not immediately alterable.[75]

Function: GUIDING

Definition:

► Assisting perplexed persons to make confident choices...when such choices are viewed as affecting the present and future state of the soul.[76]

► Helping persons in trouble make confident choices between alternative courses of action that will help them solve the problems they are facing.[77]

Ways Historically Implemented:

► Historically, pastoral guidance has been primarily inductive, at various times involving devil craft, advice giving, spiritual direction and listening.

► Helping a person in crisis requires choosing positive, healthy crisis-coping mechanisms.

Function: RECONCILING

Definition:

- Seeks to *reestablish broken relationships* between people and between individuals and God.[78]
- Seeks to reestablish broken relationships between a person and God on the one hand, and between a person and other persons on the other.[79]

Ways Historically Implemented:

- Historically, the function of reconciliation has involved such activities as forgiveness, discipline, penance, confession, and absolution.[80]

The approach I shall suggest in the following pages may border on being entirely theoretical or may suggest an approach comparable to the original intended meaning of pastoral care. Dr. Edward Wimberly, professor of Pastoral Care and Counseling at the Inter-Denominational Theological Center in Atlanta, Georgia, states:

> Pastoral Care is a communal concept. It exists whenever persons minister one to another in the name of God. In this light pastoral care is not a new concept but has its theological roots in the Judeo-Christian tradition.[81]

This statement suggests that pastoral care develops in the context of community and, in particular, the Christian community or community of faith.

My contention is that pastoral care is caring for all members of the body of Christ in the spirit of Christ. This compassion takes place through the people of the community finding identification and kinship amid their crises. I believe this caring is essential for the purpose and work of pastoral care in the African American church.

I mean to suggest here a system through which the individual's experiences create a kinship. Subsequently, caring becomes relational based upon the collective stories of the people as members of the community.

Using spirituals and hymns as tools of pastoral care in crisis intervention presents a method that is not far removed from the views held by Clebsch and Jaekle. The way these expressions are used aims at the same desired results as those by Clebsch and Jaekle regarding pastoral care. The aim and purpose of the spirituals and hymns of the African American community support each of the four functions outlined by Clebsch and Jaekle.

Notice the similarities between the four functions of pastoral care and the spirituals, which I will identify as the four functions of the spirituals and hymns of the African American church. These functions will retain the same name as their counterpart.

Function of Pastoral Care:
Healing:

The pastoral function that "aims to overcome some impairment by restoring a person to wholeness and by leading him to advance beyond his previous condition.[82]

Function of Spirituals and Hymns:
Healing:

This function of the spirituals (like pastoral care) aims at helping the individual to overcome some impairment. To this goal, I also add condition or crisis. This occurs by leading the individual(s) to advance through the lyrics of the music beyond their current state. This is the basis of the collective eschatology existing in many African American spirituals and hymns.

Function of Pastoral Care:
Sustaining:

The function that helps individuals endure and rise above situations in which a restoration to their previous condition is unlikely.[83]

Function of Spirituals and Hymns:
Sustaining:

This function of the spirituals and hymns gives encouragement, inspires hope, and engenders confidence within the individual. The individual believes that he is able to rise above his situation, knowing it may never change, but stands firm not allowing the crisis to keep him down.

Function of Pastoral Care:
Guiding:

Assisting perplexed persons to make confident choices...when such choices are viewed as affecting the present and future state of the soul.[84]

Function of Spirituals and Hymns:
Guiding:

In a time when certain choices were not available, others were. This function of the spirituals and hymns challenges the individual to choose between the righteousness of God and the wickedness of men. When evil for evil could be the order of the day between the slave and his master, the choice is made to believe God. This choice is embraced because of the individual's belief that God is involved in the individual's present and future state.

Function of Pastoral Care:
Reconciling:

Seeks to reestablish broken relationships between people and between individuals and God.[85]

Function of Spirituals and Hymns:
Reconciling:

This function of the spirituals and hymns serve to reconnect the disenfranchised and dislocated people with the larger community of faith. The emphasis addressed the individual's relationship with God and one another.

My contention is that spirituals and hymns address the same functions as given by Clebsch and Jaekle. This view suggests that spirituals and hymns represent a musical form of pastoral care; however, the administration of this approach is inherently more difficult to implement.

As tools of pastoral care in the African American community, spirituals and hymns speak of the history, hope, and freedom in African American eschatology.

Hope in African-American Christianity has more than one dimension. It is multidimensional because the liberation that the Gospel proclaims is multidimensional. Hope has a personal dimension. This aspect of hope is the focus of Christian affirmations regarding the resurrection of the body, immortality, and eternal life...Despite the abuses, the personal dimension of hope suggests that only those who truly value life and its beauty can fully appreciate the significance of resurrection. This means that pessimism is incompatible with belief in resurrection.

Resurrection does not primarily refer to a sensationalist re-composition of decaying flesh, because, as African traditional thought suggests, we are more than flesh. The body is the unity of spirit and the flesh. Resurrection, in black religious experience, points to the survival of the personality beyond death, and one's continuing existence in the presence of God and the company of the saints. Hope also has a collective or interpersonal dimension. This aspect of hope is the content of Christian belief in heaven and hell, damnation and reward. Heaven, in African-American religious thought, usually refers to being in community with others, while hell is often described as a state of alienation, not only from God, but from others. Since in African traditional thought, one's being is intimately related to the community, to be separated from solidarity with others is tantamount to nonexistence. Likewise, one's continued existence is tied to one's ongoing participation in community.[86]

The form of the spirituals and hymns in crisis intervention, I am suggesting, is like the approach stated by Donald Capps. His process developed involving the following steps: 1) Address to God, 2) Complaint, 3) Confession of trust, 4) Petition, 5) Words of assurance, and 6) Vow to praise.[87] However, the model I suggest existing in spirituals and hymns would include the following:

1) **Statement of Condition**. This component is comparable to the address to God but has its focus on identifying the crisis or condition of the individual.

2) **Admonition**. This detail involves warning, counsel, instructions, and advice given in musical form to the individual regarding his conduct, perseverance, etc., during his crisis.

3) **Encouragement.** This essential element in the spiritual and hymns engenders faith, hope, and trust that God will intervene and concentrate on the pains, problems, and troubles faced in the crisis.

4) **Anticipation of Liberation.** This element expresses the confident expectation that things wrong will be made right, even suggesting that the sufferings endured from grief and loss have in the end a future event that makes every trial and experience fit in its proper place. An anticipation of liberation speaks of a cosmology of the African American church that is pertinent to African American spirituality as a practice of human freedom.

5) **Praise and the Promise Claimed.** Another aspect found in the spirituals and hymns is a note of praise based upon the promise of God to deliver.

This basic form is present in many of the spirituals and hymns of the African American church. I believe a favorite song of the African American church that reflects this form is the song titled "Never Alone." An example of this model is found in this first verse and chorus.

I've seen the lightning flashing
And heard the thunder roll,
I've felt sin's breakers dashing,
Which tried to conquer my soul;
I've heard the voice of Jesus,
Telling me still to fight on,
He promised never to leave me,
Never to leave me alone.

CHORUS:
No, never alone,

No never alone;
He promised never to leave me,
Never to leave me alone.

The use of this model may be indigenous to the African American community and therefore not as easily transferable to others ethnic groups as are the psalms of lament. Individuals removed from the community of suffering, pain, and deliverance as experienced by the slaves may have difficulty relating to the expressions of these songs. However, I believe that the preceding form serves as a model to begin the work of intervention using spirituals and hymns and tools in crisis.

Throughout this analysis, I have intended to show that the spirituals and hymns of the African American church can guide an individual through a process that will result in regaining balance in life regardless of the loss. What I suggest is that spirituals and hymns are helpful in setting the direction or overall goal of the intervention session. Secondly, I believe that spirituals and hymns help define the role of the counselor or facilitator in the intervention. Finally, I suggest that the spirituals and hymns are useful in directing the individual back into community to find comfort in the community of fellow strugglers. Furthermore, the spirituals and hymns assist them in turning to God and finding a new relationship with Him and the strength to "press on."

ARE THE HYMNS
AND SPIRITUALS GONE?

In many of today's twenty-first century churches with their emphasis on praise and worship, contemporary, gospel music and other forms of music in the church, the singing of hymns and spirituals as a musical genre is not a regular occurrence. In some churches hymns and spirituals have been eliminated from the musical repertoire and are no longer used. The present generation is not as steeped in the traditional hymns and spirituals sung by previous generations.

The most widely used form of musical genre in the church today is contemporary praise and worship. My observation is that many contemporary praise and worship songs focus on the idea of expressing gratitude to God and appreciation for the love for God, as opposed to hymns and spirituals such as psalms of lament which are the cries of those seeking God's help in their crisis or time of distress. Praising God; giving gratitude to God; thanking God for His mercy, grace and forgiveness; and celebrating His steadfast love are dominant themes in most contemporary praise and worship songs. These themes seem to ignore, overlook, or disregard the issues that individuals may be facing in life and highlights the idea that people need more individualistic affirmations that focus more on their need to feel loved, forgiven, and accepted by God.

The hymns and spirituals like the psalms of lament did not focus on acceptance, forgiveness, or the need to feel loved. These songs expressed the belief of the individuals or communities that they were already loved, accepted, and forgiven by God. They believed that God was on the side of the persecuted and oppressed, and expressed confidence that because of the unconditional love of God, His acceptance, and His forgiveness, that He would indeed act on behalf of His people.

Most contemporary praise and worship songs are not written with the intent of asking God for help during distress. They are written in a current and personal style that relates more to a relationship with God as opposed to calling upon God during times of pain and confusion. Many praise and worship songs do not include a hopeful conclusion in which a trust is expressed in God for hearing the prayers of His people and delivering them from their crises.

In his book *The Spirituality of the Psalms*, Old Testament scholar Walter Brueggemann argued that the absence of lament in our communal worship was a symptom of exactly how much in bondage the church was to Western culture's triumphalist narratives of health and wealth. He suggests that we are quicker to declare final victory and imminent triumph than mourn present reality.

Perhaps this trend is growing in many communities; however, I don't believe this shift explores the need for people in crisis to address their situation or receive a level of care or healing in their situation. Amid the many crises and issues faced in life, grieving is a necessary part of our experience. People need to grieve. Like the psalmists and the writers of the many hymns and spirituals, we need to name what we are facing, identify our struggles and pains, and recognize it for what it is.

Currently, our country is still emerging from the impact of a global pandemic. As a result of this global crisis, people were affected physically, financially, mentally, spiritually and emotionally. Families were disrupted by sudden deaths and other serious life changes. The work environment was affected, and social life was disrupted. Adults and children alike and people from all walks of life were thrown into crisis. What was considered a "normal" life was now far from normal. Disruption was the new normal. This pandemic disruption of our daily lives could have been the impetus to push people into a national cry for the deliverance of God from our distress, expressing our grief, disorientation, and sense of loss, causing us to yearn for and seek the intervention and deliverance of God. This motivation, however, did not prove to be the case; rather, instead served as a crisis that propelled man to become more self-centered and concerned about his own well-being leading him to seek man's solutions to the crises now faced.

Such may be the case within the church because contemporary worship music lacks a significant number of songs focused on suffering. The themes of suffering are scarcely present in the repertoire of modern worship songs. Today we don't really have many songs of laments to sing.

REPRESSED GRIEF OR "JUST GET OVER IT"

In view of the absence of or little use of spirituals and hymns in the church, I wonder if the church is dealing with a repression of grief, or if we have adopted a just-get-over-it-and-move-on attitude. Perhaps our modern praise and worship songs cause us to seek to get past or get over our crisis with human wisdom or strength rather than trust God to deliver us in our crises.

The fact is crises exist and always will. People still look for ways to address, cope with, or manage their personal situations. I believe that the same need is still present, and pastoral care of people in crisis is relevant and necessary even more today. The crisis in mental health, school shootings, disasters, terrorism, and more has presented many challenges for the church to address in the lives of its congregation and the community. My belief is that pastoral care does not mean pastoral cure. The ministry of care is providing people in crisis with the caring ministry of the church using its available resources. These resources include the many hymns and spirituals sung by people of faith expressing their trust and confidence in their God.

Many of the songs of this generation unlike the hymns, spirituals, and psalms of lament do not seek to express the pain and hurts of the grief or crisis faced. Neither do they conclude with a vow to trust God or affirming a faith and hope in God. They often end with self-reliance, self-hope, and other comparable ideas rooted in soulish dependence on personal ability. This independence rooted in the soul of man, his mind, will, and emotions is disconnected to a spiritual resolve to trust God.

Failure to recognize or acknowledge our grief suppresses truth and eventually numbs our emotions. People who are not allowed to grieve could eventually lose or become disconnected from their ability to even express joy. I believe that if we do not mourn in our grief and our crisis and sorrow over those things that grieve the heart of God, we become less likely to be true representatives of His grace and His deliverance. We then fail to acknowledge God as our Source and Deliverer Who comforts, heals, and gives hope through our crisis.

A Final Word

This final word is not meant as a condemnation of our contemporary praise and worship songs. Each of our contemporary praise and worship songs express a heart for God, a love for God, and a passion for a relationship with God. I refer to them because they are significant.

And each generation represents differing styles and genres in music, praise, worship, and sharing their hope. I only seek to acknowledge the difference between the contemporary praise and worship music used in the church today and the spirituals and hymns used in the church historically. The latter gave a dimension of hope, trust, and confidence for individuals going through crisis, pain, grief, or other situations that necessitated the intervention of God.

In consideration of the widespread use of contemporary praise and worship music and the lack of the use of hymns and spirituals, my assertion is that the hymns and spirituals of the church are still viable tools in the ministry of care. Psalms and hymns can still be used in church as tools of pastoral care for people in grief or crisis. Contemporary praise and worship music has its place in the worship experience for the worshipper; however, in many cases they fall short of the care and hope that is needed. The deliverance to be found in trusting God is essential to the well-being sought by the individuals during their crisis.

My belief is that the church would do well to incorporate these hymns and spirituals regardless of ethnic origin or community. All communities of faith have relied on and used many spirituals and hymns—not because of their ethnicity or their community of origin, but because of the people being companions in crisis and suffering. Crisis knows no race, creed, or color. Grief knows no race, creed, or color. Neither crisis nor grief are restricted nor limited to any cultural group, class of people, or age, affecting all who live. And because of this fact, I believe that the reinsertion of spirituals and hymns would serve greatly as an effective tool in caring for the members of congregations and communities to bring about healing, guiding, sustaining, and restorating of troubled souls. These four functions of pastoral care are often manifest in the hymns and spirituals of the local church.

Civilla Durfee Holden Martin, a Canadian American writer of

many religious hymns and gospel songs in the late nineteenth and early twentieth century, was inspired by the words of Jesus from the gospel of Matthew 10:29-31:

> *Are not two sparrows sold for a farthing? and one of them shall not fall on the ground without your Father.* *30But the very hairs of your head are all numbered.* *31Fear ye not therefore, ye are of more value than many sparrows.*

An article written by C. Michael Hawn, who served as University Distinguished Professor of Church Music and director of the Sacred Music program at Perkins School of Theology at Southern Methodist University in Dallas, Texas, references the context out of which the hymn was born. In summary, he shares a story regarding Mrs. Martin's experience with Mr. and Mrs. Doolittle who were very dear friends. Mrs. Doolittle had been bedridden for years, and her husband was an incurable cripple. However, regardless of their afflictions, they lived happy Christian lives, giving inspiration and comfort to all who knew them.

One day while the Martins were visiting the Doolittles, Civilla's husband asked the couple what the secret was to their bright hopefulness amid the crises that they continually suffered. Mrs. Doolittle's response was simple: "His eye is on the sparrow, and I know He watches me." This statement resonated in Civilla Martin's heart, stimulated her thinking, and the hymn "His Eye Is on the Sparrow" was born.

> *Why should I feel discouraged? Why should the shadows come?*
> *Why should my heart be lonely and long for heaven and home?*
> *When Jesus is my portion? My constant friend is he;*
> *His eye is on the sparrow, and I know he watches me.*

The themes of finding comfort amidst grief or crisis and feeling watched over by Jesus, Who is described as a "constant friend," provided comfort and hope to the African American community during the Civil Rights movement. I believe that African American gospel artist Kirk Franklin's inspiration came from Martin's song when he composed "Why We Sing." The chorus reinforces this theme with the lines—"I sing because I'm happy, I sing because I'm free"—which resonated with many, particularly African Americans, inspiring great hope for deliverance from the crises faced by a community.

If there is a time when these spirituals and hymns are needful and useful as tools of pastoral care in all communities, that time is now!

QUESTIONNAIRE
Hymns and Spirituals as Tools of Pastoral Care

Instructions:

This questionnaire is designed to assess your use of spirituals and hymns, whether traditional or contemporary arrangements, as ways of helping you cope with, handle, or survive crisis or grief experiences in your life. As you complete this information, be mindful of the definitions of the words *grief* and *crisis* as used in this questionnaire.

Observe the following definitions:

► In this questionnaire, *crisis* means "a crucial time or a turning point." Two basic types of crises are *developmental* and *situational*.[87]

    a. *Developmental* crises are "the predictable experiences that everyone goes through in the process of maturity."

    b. Situational crises are "exceptional and unpredictable resulting from unusual circumstances such as divorce, death, and loss of job or disabling accident." Situational crises might arise in connection with loss of a job, of a support person, or of a position of status and respect. The discovery of marital infidelity, retirement, an unwanted pregnancy, moving to a new city, the diagnosis of a life-threatening disease, rape or incest, or a home burglary are other examples of situational crises. The list is extensive, including any event that poses a serious threat to a person or a family that may lead to a situational crisis.

▶ In this questionnaire, *grief* means "a normal and natural response to loss." Grief is a mixture of emotions experienced following any major change in a familiar or routine pattern of behavior or life. We grieve the loss of relationships. Moving from one house or city to another may cause grief. Marriage or divorce can cause feelings of loss and result in a time of grief. Retirement, children growing up and leaving home, loss of health and more often contribute to a grief response.

Personal Data
Gender ☐ Male ☐ Female
Your Age: _____

Grief Experience
1. What kinds of crises and losses have you experienced?
   (Check all that apply; list others in the space provided.)

   ☐ Death of a parent   ☐ Loss of a job

   ☐ Retirement   ☐ Loss of health

   ☐ Loss of a friend   ☐ Divorce

   ☐ Loss of an ability   ☐ Loss of a home

   ☐ Death of spouse   ☐ Loss of transportation

   ☐ Relocation to another city

2. What feelings of grief did you experience during your times of crisis and loss? *(Check all that apply.)*

   ☐ Anger ☐ Fear ☐ Depression

   ☐ Worry ☐ Denial ☐ Isolation

   ☐ Loneliness ☐ Physical illness ☐ Loss of appetite

   ☐ Bitterness ☐ Regret ☐ Sadness

   ☐ Other _____

   ☐ Other _____

   ☐ Other _____

3. In the experience of your crises and losses did particular hymns or spiritual songs give you comfort or help you deal with the feelings you experienced?

   ☐ Yes ☐ No

4. In the space provided, include the name of the song if you remember it. Or write the words of that song that you remember giving you comfort or strength during your crisis or grief experience. *(Use additional paper if necessary.)*

   _____

   _____

   _____

   _____

   _____

   _____

5. Select one of the songs given and state how this song gave you comfort and strength during your time of crisis.

_____

_____

_____

_____

_____

_____

6. List or write any Scriptures from the Bible that were helpful to you during your times of crisis and loss.

_____

_____

_____

_____

_____

_____

7. In the following list of songs, check the ones that have sustained you, given you guidance and healing, or have assisted you in reconciling your loss in a crisis time or a time of grief.

☐ "I Trust in God" ☐ "Close to Thee"
☐ "Leave It There" ☐ "Amazing Grace"
☐ "Stand By Me" ☐ "It Is Well with My Soul"
☐ "God Will Take Care of You"

☐ "I Need Thee Every Hour"
☐ "Great Gettin' Up Morning"
☐ "Precious Lord, Take My Hand"
☐ "What a Friend We Have in Jesus"
☐ "We'll Understand It Better By and By"
☐ "God Leads His Dear Children Along"
☐ "Soon Ah Will Be Done with de Troubles of the World "

8. In the space provided, list any other songs that were instrumental in giving you strength, support, and encouragement during your times of crisis and loss.

_____

_____

_____

_____

_____

END NOTES

PREFACE

[1]Howard Stone, *Crisis Counseling: Creative Pastoral Care and Counseling* (Minneapolis: Fortress Press, 1993), 23.

[2]Ibid., 25.

[3]Donald Capps, *Biblical Approaches to Pastoral Counseling* (Philadelphia: Westminster Press, 1981), 49.

THE DEVELOPMENT OF AFRICAN AMERICAN SPIRITUALS AND HYMNS

[1]James H. Cone, *The Spirituals and the Blues: An Interpretation* (New York: The Seabury Press, Inc., 1972), 5.

[2]J. Wendell Mapson Jr., *The Ministry of Music in the Black Church* (Philadelphia: Judson Press, 1984), 23.

[3]Dwight N. Hopkins. *Shoes that Fit Our Feet: Sources for a Constructive Black Theology* (New York: Orbis Books, 1993), 13.

[4]Miles Mark Fisher, *Negro Songs in the United States* (Ithaca: Cornell University Press, 1953), 5-6.

[5]Hopkins, 114.

[6]Ibid., 114-15.

[7]Jeremiah Wright, "Music in the Black Church," Lecture.

[8]Cone, 5.

[9]Ibid., 5.

[10]Ibid., 6.

[11]Hopkins, 47.

[12]Wyatt Tee Walker, *Somebody's Calling My Name: Black Sacred Music and Social Change* (Valley Forge: Judson Press, 1972), 7-9.

[13]Willi Apel, *Harvard Dictionary of Music* (Cambridge: Harvard University Press, 1977), 397.

[14]Geoffrey Hindley, ed., *The Larousse Encyclopedia of Music* (Secaucus, N. J.: Chartwell Books, 1976), 60.

[15]Eileen Southern, *The Music of Black Americans* (New York: W. W. Norton, 1971), 40.

[16]J. Jefferson Cleveland et al, *Songs of Zion* (Nashville: Abingdon Press, 1981), 2.

[17]Tony Heilbut, The Gospel Sound (New York: Simon & Schuster, 1971), pp. 58.

[18]J. Jefferson Cleveland et al, *Songs of Zion* (Nashville: Abingdon Press, 1981).

[19]Mapson Jr., 36.

[20]Cleveland, 73.

[21]Cone, 34-35.

[22]This paraphrase represents a personal adaptation of John 1.

[23]John W. James and Frank Cherry, *The Grief Recovery Handbook: A Step-by-Step Program for Moving Beyond Loss* (New York: Harper Perennial Publishers, 1988), 3-4.

[24]R. A. DeVaul and Sidney Zisook, "Unresolved Grief: Clinical Considerations," *Postgraduate Medicine*, 1961, Vol. 59, 267-71.

[25]Howard W. Stone, *Suicide and Grief* (Philadelphia: Fortress Press, 1972).

[26]Howard Clinebell, *Basic Types of Pastoral Care & Counseling: Resources for the Ministry of Healing and Growth* (Nashville: Abingdon Press, 1984), 219.

[27]Jess Stein, ed., *The Random House College Dictionary*, Rev. ed. (New York: Random House, 1975).

[28]Stephen Breck Reid, *Listening In: A Multicultural Reading of the Psalms*. (Nashville: Abingdon Press, 1997), 8-9.

[29]Ibid, 9.

[30]Rodney J. Hunter, ed., *Dictionary of Pastoral Care and Counseling* (Nashville: Abingdon Press, 1990).

[31]Walter Brueggemann, *The Message of the Psalms: A Theological Commentary* (Minneapolis: Augsburg Publishing House, 1984), 19-23.

[32]J. David Pleins, *The Psalms: Songs of Tragedy, Hope, and Justice* (New York: Orbis Books, 1993), 9.

[33]Ibid., 9.

[34]Brueggemann, 54-57.

[35]Claus Westermann, *Praise and Lament in the Psalms* (Atlanta: John Knox Press, 1973), 33, 64.

[36]Capps, 60.

[37]Bernhard W. Anderson, *Out of the Depths: The Psalms Speak for Us Today* (Westminster Press, 1970) quotee in Capps, *Biblical Approaches to Pastoral Counseling*, 60-61.

[38]Westermann.

[39]Ann Weems, *Psalms of Lament* (Louisville: Westminster John Knox Press, 1995), xvi –xvii.

[40]George A. Lindbeck, *The Nature of Doctrine: religion and Theology in a Postliberal Age* (Philadelphia: Westminster Press, 1984), 34.

[41]Ann Streaty Wimberly, *Soul Stories: African American Christian Education* (Nashville: Abingdon Press, 1994), 39.

[42]Glen R. Hufnagel, *Spirituals and Poetry in Catholic Worship, Freeing the Spirit 7*, no. 1, (Spring 1981), 23.

[43]Ibid.

[44]Cone, 108.

[45]Ibid, 119.

[46]Hildred Roach, *Black American Music: Past and Present* (Boston: Crescendo Publishing Co., 1973), 26.

[47]Hufnagel, 23.

[48]Ibid.

[49]Ibid.

[50]Ibid.

[51]Capps, 47-48.

[52]Ibid., 91-92.

[53]Karl Slaikeu and Steve Lawhead, *The Phoenix Factor: Surviving and Growing Through Personal Crisis* (Boston: Houghton Mifflin Co., 1985), 1-2.

[54]Ibid.

[55]Stone, 13.

[56]Gerald Caplan, *An Approach to Community Mental Health* (New York: Grune & Stratton, 1966), 14.

[57]Stone, 13.

[58]Ibid., 17.

[59]Hopkins, 13.

[60]Ibid., 15.

[61]Ibid., 17.

[62]James H. Evans Jr., *We Have Been Believers* (Minneapolis: Fortress Press, 1992), 146-47.

[63]J. Garfield Owens, *All God's Chillun: Meditations on Negro Spirituals* (Nashville: Abingdon Press, 1971), 13-17.

[64]Deloris Williams, *Sisters in the Wilderness* (New York: Orbis Press, 1993), 6.

[65]Evans Jr., 152.

[66]Wyatt Tee Walker, *The Soul of Black Worship: A Trilogy* (New York: Martin Luther King Fellows Press, 1986), 47-85.

[67]McKim, Donald K., *Westminster Dictionary of Theological Terms* (Louisville: Westminster John Knox Press, 1996).

[68]William A. Clebsch and Charles R. Jaekle, *Pastoral Care in Historical Perspective* (New Jersey: Prentice-Hall. 1964).

[69]Clebsch and Jaekle.

[70]Edward P. Wimberly, *Pastoral Care in the Black Church* (Nashville: Abingdon Press, 1979).

[71]Clebsch and Jaekle.

[72]Clebsch and Jaekle.

[73]Wimberly.

[74]Clebsch and Jaekle.

[75]Wimberly.

[76]Clebsch and Jaekle.

[77]Wimberly.

[78]Clebsch and Jaekle.

[79]Wimberly.

[80]Clebsch and Jaekle.

[81]Wimberly.

[82]Clebsch and Jaekle.

[83]Clebsch and Jaekle.

[84]Clebsch and Jaekle.

[85]Clebsch and Jaekle.

[86]Evans Jr., 153-54.

[87]Capps.

[88]Stone, *Crisis Counseling*, 13-14.

END NOTES

Anderson, Gary A. *A Time to Mourn, A Time to Dance: The Expression of Grief and Joy in Israelite Religion.* University Park: Pennsylvania State University Press, 1991.

Apel, Willi. *Harvard Dictionary of Music.* Cambridge: Harvard University Press, 1977.

Borchert, Gerald L. and Andrew D. Lester, eds. *Spiritual Dimensions of Pastoral Care.* Philadelphia: Westminster Press, 1985.

Brister, C. W. *Change Happens: Finding Your Way Through Life's Transitions.* Macon: Peake Road Press, 1997.

Brueggemann, Walter. *The Message of the Psalms.* Minneapolis: Augsburg Publishing House, 1984.

_____. *The Psalms and the Life of Faith.* Minneapolis: Fortress Press, 1995.

Caplan, Gerald. *An Approach to Community Mental Health.* New York: Grune & Stratton Publishing, 1966.

Capps, Donald. *Biblical Approaches to Pastoral Counseling.* Philadelphia: Westminster Press, 1981.

Clebsch, William A. and Charles R. Jaekle, *Pastoral Care in Historical Perspective.* New Jersey: Prentice-Hall. 1964.

Cleveland, J. Jefferson et al, *Songs of Zion*. Nashville: Abingdon Press, 1981.

Clinebell, Howard. *Basic Types of Pastoral Care & Counseling: Resources for the Ministry of Healing and Growth*. Nashville: Abingdon Press, 1984.

Cone, James H. *The Spirituals and the Blues: An Interpretation*. Seabury Press: New York, 1972.

DeVaul, R. A. and Sidney Zisook, "Unresolved Grief: Clinical Considerations," *Postgraduate Medicine*, 1961, Vol. 59.

Dixon, Christa K. *Negro Spirituals: From Bible to Folksong*. Philadelphia: Fortress Press, 1976.

Evans Jr., James H. *We Have Been Believers*. Minneapolis: Fortress Press, 1992.

Fisher, Miles Mark. *Negro Songs in the United States*. Ithaca: Cornell University Press, 1953.

Fowler, James W. *Faithful Change: The Personal and Public Challenges of Postmodern Life*. Nashville: Abingdon Press, 1996.

Heilbut, Tony. *The Gospel Sound*. New York: Simon & Schuster, 1971.

Hindley, Geoffrey, ed. *The Larousse Encyclopedia of Music*. Secaucus, N. J.: Chartwell Books, 1976.

Hopkins, Dwight N. *Shoes that Fit Our Feet: Sources for a Constructive Black Theology*. New York: Orbis Books, 1993.

James, John W., and Cherry, Frank. *The Grief Recovery Handbook: A Step-by-Step Program for Moving Beyond Loss*. HarperPerennial: New York, 1988.

Kennedy, Eugene. *Crisis Counseling: The Essential Guide for Nonprofessional Counselors*. New York: Continuum International Publishing Group, 1989.

Keough, G. Arthur. *Rejoicing with the Psalmist*. Boise: Pacific Press Publishing Association, 1990.

Lester, Andrew D. *Hope in Pastoral Care and Counseling*. Louisville: Westminster John Knox Press, 1995.

Lovell Jr., John. *Black Song: The Forge and the Flame*. New York: Macmillian Company, 1972.

Mapson Jr., J. Wendell. *The Ministry of Music in the Black Church*. Philadelphia: Judson Press, 1984.

McKim, Donald K., *Westminster Dictionary of Theological Terms*. Louisville: Westminster John Knox Press, 1996.

Mitchell, Henry H. *Soul Theology*. San Francisco: Harper and Row, Publishers, 1986.

Oates, Wayne E. *The Christian Pastor*. Philadelphia: Westminster Press, 1982.

Owens, J. Garfield. *All God's Chillun: Meditations on Negro Spirituals*. Nashville: Abingdon Press, 1971.

Pleins, J. David. *The Psalms: Songs of Tragedy, Hope, and Justice*. Maryknoll, N.Y.: Orbis Books, 1993.

Reid, Stephen Breck. *Listening In: A Multicultural Reading of the Psalms*. Nashville: Abingdon Press, 1997.

Roach, Hildred. *Black American Music: Past and Present*. Boston: Crescendo Publishing Co., 1973.

Slaikeu, Karl and Steve Lawhead. *The Phoenix Factor: Surviving and Growing Through Personal Crisis.* Boston: Houghton Mifflin Co., 1985.

Southern, Eileen. *The Music of Black Americans.* New York: W. W. Norton, 1971.

Spencer, Jon Michael. *Black Hymnody: A Hymnological History of the African-American Church.* Knoxville: University of Tennessee Press, 1992.

_____. *Sing a New Song: Liberating Black Hymnody.* Minneapolis: Fortress Press, 1995.

Stewart III, Carlyle Fielding. *African American Church Growth: 12 Principles for Prophetic Ministry.* Nashville: Abingdon Press, 1994.

_____. *Soul Survivors: An African-American Spirituality.* Louisville: Westminster John Knox Press, 1997.

Stone, Howard. *Crisis Counseling.* Minneapolis: Fortress Press, 1993.

_____. *Suicide and Grief.* Philadelphia: Fortress Press, 1972.

Switzer, David K. *The Minister As Crisis Counselor.* Nashville: Abingdon Press, 1974.

Thurman, Howard. *Deep River: Reflections on the Religious Insight of Certain Negro Spirituals.* New York: Harper & Brothers, 1955.

Walker, Wyatt Tee. *Somebody's Calling My Name: Black Sacred Music and Social Change.* Valley Forge: Judson Press, 1972.

_____. *The Soul of Black Worship: A Trilogy.* New York: Martin Luther King Fellows Press, 1986.

Westermann, Claus. *Praise and Lament in the Psalms.* Atlanta: John Knox Press, 1981.

Williams, Deloris. *Sisters in the Wilderness.* New York: Orbis Press, 1993.

Wimberly, Edward P., *African American Pastoral Care.* Nashville: Abingdon Press, 1992.

Wright, Jeremiah. "Music in the Black Church." Lecture.

Wright, H. Norman. *Crisis Counseling: A Practical Guide for Pastors, Counselors and Friends.* Ventura: Regal Books, 1993.

www.ingramcontent.com/pod-product-compliance
Lightning Source LLC
Chambersburg PA
CBHW071353090426
42738CB00012B/3105